Legends of the Frontier: Daniel Boone, Davy Crockett and Jim Bowie

By Charles River Editors

Portrait of Daniel Boone by John James Audubon

About Charles River Editors

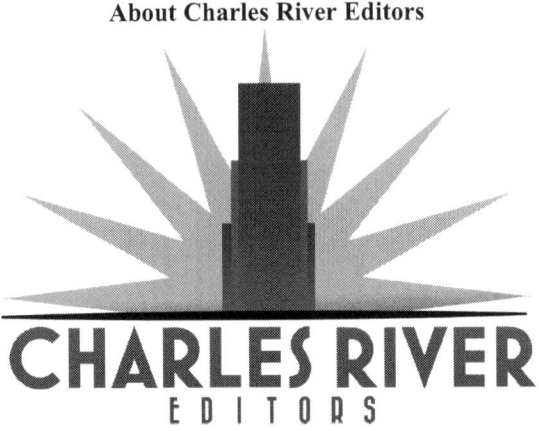

Charles River Editors was founded by Harvard and MIT alumni to provide superior editing and original writing services, with the expertise to create digital content for publishers across a vast range of subject matter. In addition to providing original digital content for third party publishers, Charles River Editors republishes civilization's greatest literary works, bringing them to a new generation via ebooks.

Introduction

Daniel Boone (1734-1820)

"Many heroic actions and chivalrous adventures are related of me which exist only in the regions of fancy. With me the world has taken great liberties, and yet I have been but a common man." – Daniel Boone

A lot of ink has been spilled covering the lives of history's most influential figures, but how much of the forest is lost for the trees? In Charles River Editors' American Legends series, readers can get caught up to speed on the lives of America's most important men and women in the time it takes to finish a commute, while learning interesting facts long forgotten or never known.

The Wild West and the frontier have long held a special place in the narrative of American history, and all of the legends and folk heroes who lived in the 19th century owe their reputation to the original American frontier folk hero, Daniel Boone. Boone was literally a trailblazer: the legendary pioneer established his Wilderness Road by striking west into present-day Kentucky and establishing Boonesborough, one of the earliest white settlements west of the Appalachians. Hundreds of thousands of settlers would follow his path by the end of the 18th century.

While that was an important and proud legacy for the former Revolutionary War militiaman and Virginia State Assemblyman, Boone became known for the outsized tales and adventures associated with his foray into the frontier. Far and wide, people spoke of Boone's expert marksmanship, his encounters with wild bears, and his hardscrabble frontier life, making him a living legend and the prototypical Western frontier folk hero in America. All of it bewildered and bemused the actual man himself, whose own words about his affinity for the backwoods made him sound more like Henry David Thoreau than anything else. Boone once noted, "Situated, many hundred miles from our families in the howling wilderness, I believe few would have equally enjoyed the happiness we experienced. I often observed to my brother, You see now how little nature requires to be satisfied. Felicity, the companion of content, is rather found in our own breasts than in the enjoyment of external things…"

Of course, that's how nobody has chosen to remember Daniel Boone, and the legends and lore have long outstripped the man himself. The legend of Daniel Boone helped him become an inspiration and model for Americans on the frontier, while also serving to make him the embodiment of the American pioneer overseas. Lord Byron even mentions Boone in his classic *Don Juan* (Of the great names which in our faces stare,/The General Boon, back-woodsman of Kentucky/Was happiest amongst mortals any where;/For killing nothing but a bear or buck, he/Enjoyed the lonely vigorous, harmless days/ Of his old age in wilds of deepest maze.")

Legends of the Frontier chronicles the life of the frontier hero, and the legends and mythmaking that have shaped his legacy. Along with pictures of important people, places, and events, you will learn about America's original frontier folk hero like you never have before, in no time at all.

Davy Crockett (1786-1836)

"I know not whether, in the eyes of the world, a brilliant death is not preferred to an obscure life of rectitude. Most men are remembered as they died, and not as they lived. We gaze with admiration upon the glories of the setting sun, yet scarcely bestow a passing glance upon its noonday splendor." – Davy Crockett

The Wild West and the frontier have long held a special place in the narrative of American history, and of all the legends and folk heroes who lived in the 19th century, none became as famous as Davy Crockett, "The King of the Wild Frontier".

Crockett had the distinction of being a living legend in his own life. Known as a hardscrabble frontiersman who could spin a good yarn but who also took a no-nonsense approach that brought him from the backwoods of Tennessee to the halls of Congress. Though he served during the presidency of another Westerner, Andrew Jackson, Crockett was very much his own man, and he was distrustful of other politicians, a sentiment that has only endured him further to subsequent generations of Americans.

In 1834, Crockett was promoting his autobiography, which provided colorful accounts of his life on the frontier, all while facing reelection. In the midst of the campaign, Crockett noted, "I told the people of my district that I would serve them as faithfully as I had done; but if not ... you may all go to hell, and I will go to Texas." When he lost in 1834, he kept his word and set off for Texas, a spot he grew to love so much that he would write to his children in 1836, "I must say as to what I have seen of Texas, it is the garden spot of the world. The best land & best prospects for health I ever saw is here, and I do believe it is a fortune to any man to come here. There is a world of country to settle."

Crockett was famous in his lifetime, but it was his death in Texas that made him an American legend. Though there is still some mystery and controversy surrounding exactly what transpired at the Battle of the Alamo, the deaths of Crockett, Travis, Bowie and the rest of the defenders at the hands of Santa Anna's Mexican soldiers became a symbol of sacrifice and defiance, and the battle itself became a rallying cry throughout the rest of Texas' War for Independence. Naturally, it also cemented Crockett's legacy as well.

Legends of the Frontier looks at the amazing life of the frontier hero, his controversial death, and the fantastic legends and mythmaking that have shaped his legacy. Along with pictures of important people, places, and events, you will learn about The King of the Wild Frontier like you never have before, in no time at all.

Jim Bowie (1796-1836)

"I'll wage they found no bullets in his back." - Jim Bowie's mother after hearing of his death at the Alamo

Jim Bowie is one of 19th century America's most famous names, even if what's known about the man is more legend than fact. Like Daniel Boone and Davy Crockett, Bowie has come to represent the pioneering spirit of the frontier, along with the masculinity, machismo and swagger that earned him a reputation for fighting. And like any good legend, he is perhaps best remembered for his death at the Alamo than for any aspect of his life. Bowie's death and the defenders' defeat at the Alamo did not have a decisive impact on Texas' War for Independence, but it became a poignant rallying cry in the immediate aftermath of the battle, and to this day Americans associate it with patriotism, bravery and determination. "Remember the Alamo" is still a widely used part of the English lexicon today, and the Alamo is a cherished piece of Americana.

Much of Bowie's participation in the Alamo is still controversial, and fittingly he was known across America before that for another controversy. In what became known as the notorious Sandbar Fight of 1827, a duel between two men turned into a large fight that included Bowie, who was shot and stabbed during the melee but still managed to stab to death the sheriff of Rapides Parish in Louisiana with a large knife that has since become universally known as the Bowie knife. Between that fight and his death, Bowie became one of the Western frontier's most celebrated folk heroes.

Legends of the Frontier chronicles the life, myths and legends of the frontier folk hero, examining the known and unknown in an attempt to separate fact from fiction. Along with pictures of important people and places, you will learn about Bowie like you never have before, in no time at all.

Daniel Boone Escorting Settlers through the Cumberland Gap, by George Caleb Bingham (1851-1852)

Daniel Boone

Chapter 1: Early Years

The Boone Family Tree

"SOME men choose to live in crowded cities;—others are pleased with the peaceful quiet of a country farm; while some love to roam through wild forests, and make their homes in the wilderness. The man of whom I shall now speak, was one of this last class. Perhaps you never heard of Daniel Boone, the Kentucky rifleman. If not, then I have a strange and interesting story to tell you." – *The Adventures of Daniel Boone, Kentucky Rifleman*

Though he will forever be associated with the frontier, Kentucky, and Virginia, Daniel Boone was born on November 2, 1734 in a log cabin near present-day Reading, Pennsylvania, the sixth of eleven children and fourth son born to Squire and Sarah Morgan Boone, hard-working and adventurous Quaker parents. His siblings are recorded as Sarah, Israel, Samuel, Jonathan, Elizabeth, Mary, George, Edward, Squire, and Hanna. (One Boone family tradition suggests that Daniel was named after well-known dutch painter Daniel Boone—said to have been a distant relative.)

The Daniel Boone Homestead, site of his birth (the house was built over the log cabin)

The Boone family belonged to the Religious Society of Friends, better known as Quakers, a community that had made its way to Pennsylvania after suffering religious persecution in England. Daniel's grandfather, George Boone, was born in 1666 in Stoak Hamlet in Devonshire, England, with Daniel's father, Squire (born in 1696) emigrating from the small town of Bradninch, Devon (near Exeter, England) to Pennsylvania in 1713 to join William Penn's new colony (formed of other like-minded dissenters). In 1717, his parents, George and Mary Boone, joined their son in Pennsylvania.

On July 23, 1720, Squire Boone (who was a somewhat prosperous weaver and blacksmith) married Sarah Morgan (born in 1700). Sarah's family, also Quakers, settled in Towamencin Township, Montgomery County, Pennsylvania in 1708, emigrating from Wales. Squire was described as "a man of rather small stature, fair complexion, red hair, and grey eyes." Sarah was "a woman over the common size, strong and active, with black hair and eyes."[1]

In 1731, three years before Daniel's birth, the Boones moved to the Oley Valley near the modern city of Reading, Pennsylvania, where Daniel was born and spent much of his early life.

Pennsylvania Frontier

Daniel Boone was as good a selection as any to ultimately become a frontier folk hero. In addition to spending his early years on what was then the edge of the Pennsylvania frontier, where several Native American villages stood as backdrops, Daniel was inured to hard work at an early age. Maintaining a highly-driven work ethic, Daniel's parents ran a small farm, a blacksmith shop, and a weaving establishment, forcing Daniel to spend much of his childhood helping work the field.

In 1742, when Daniel was eight years of age, the noted Moravian (east of the Czech Republic) missionary Count Zinzendorf held a synod (church council) in a nearby barn which Daniel and a group of Delaware Native American Christian converts attended—further instilling in Daniel a close relationship with his "red brethren." The Boone household was a frequent gathering place for village meetings and community organizing, with local Natives usual visitors.

However, relations between the Boone family and the Quakers were about to sour. That same year, the Boone family became the focus of controversy in their little community (comprised almost exclusively of fellow Quakers) when the Boone's eldest child, Sarah, married John Willcockson, a "worldling" (non-Quaker). This arrangement compelled Squire and Sarah to publicly apologize for their daughter's transgression. Five years later, however, when Daniel's

---

[1] Thwaites (Gold) Reuben, *Daniel Boone*. Page 5.

oldest brother Israel also married a "worldling," Squire Boone further alienated himself from the community by standing by his son's decision, which led to the expulsion of the Boone family from the village. Although Daniel continued to consider himself a Christian and would see to it that all his children were baptized, he would never attend church again nor join a Quaker community.

When Daniel was ten, Squire bought an additional plot of land some distance from the main house, where Daniel took up residence with his mother. Daniel tended the cows while the "stout-armed" Sarah worked the dairy house, making butter and cheese. It was here that the young boy had to learn survival skills, self-reliance, and wood crafts, spending a great deal of time learning "Indian" ways. He is said to have mastered "stick-throwing" prior to learning to shoot, and he was able to bring down birds and other small game quite efficiently.

Receiving his first rifle at the age of twelve as a gift from his father, Daniel learned to hunt from both local settlers and Natives, beginning his lifelong love of hunting (and, of course, the folk legends that would follow him through life). In one often-repeated account, the young Daniel was hunting in the woods with some other boys when they heard the howl of a mountain lion nearby. While the other boys scattered and ran for home, Daniel is said to have calmly cocked his rifle and shot the animal cleaning through the heart--just as it was about to pounce on him. While this tale may be partly fact and partly fiction, it exemplifies the legendary status that would follow—and precede--Daniel Boone to his final days.

One mid-19th century book about Boone's life and adventures, *The Adventures of Daniel Boone, Kentucky Rifleman*, demonstrates how such frontier tales and exploits were presented to the American public in those days:

"He was scarcely able to carry a gun, when he was shooting all the squirrels, rackoons, and even wild-cats (it is said), that he could find in that region. As he grew older, his courage increased, and then we find him amusing himself with higher game. Other lads in the neighborhood were soon taught by him the use of the rifle, and were then able to join him in his adventures. On one occasion, they all started out for a hunt, and after amusing themselves till it was almost dark, were returning homeward, when suddenly a wild cry was heard in the woods. The boys screamed out, "A panther! a panther!" and ran off as fast as they could. Boone stood firmly, looking around for the animal. It was a panther indeed. His eye lighted upon him just in the act of springing toward him: in an instant he levelled his rifle, and shot him through the heart."

That same book suggests in the following paragraph that even as a boy, Daniel was capable of being entirely self-sufficient:

"But this sort of sport was not enough for him. He seemed resolved to go away from men, and live in the forests with these animals. One morning he started off as usual, with his rifle and dog. Night came on, but Daniel did not return to his home. Another day and night passed away, and still the boy did not make his appearance. His parents were now greatly alarmed. The neighbors joined them in making search for the lad. After wandering about a great while, they at length saw smoke rising from a cabin in the distance. Upon reaching it, they found the boy. The floor of the cabin was covered with the skins of such animals as he had slain, and pieces of meat were roasting before the fire for his supper. Here, at a distance of three miles from any settlement, he had built his cabin of sods and branches, and sheltered himself in the wilderness."

Daniel is also said to have acquired fair skills as a blacksmith, able to craft metal for reparation of traps and guns.

North Carolina Frontier

In 1750, Squire sold his land and moved his family by covered wagon and horseback some 500 miles to North Carolina, eventually settling on the Yadkin River in what is now Davie County, North Carolina. Thus, 16 year old Daniel and his family moved to the wild frontier along the Yadkin River in North Carolina, reaching their final destination in the fall of 1751. Once they arrived, Daniel's remarkable shooting skills (a speedy hand and keen eye honed through constant rifle practice) were used to Boone family advantage. His father tasked him with keeping the family supplied with fresh meat, while Squire and his other sons maintained the farm, smithy, and dairy. Buffalo was so plentiful in this time and place that Daniel and a few of his friends with dogs could down 10-20 of the enormous animals in a single day, or so the story goes. According to the legends, the teenager was truly the provider for his entire family:

"The old man with his other sons went busily to the work of making a farm. As for Daniel, they knew it was idle to expect his help in such employment, and therefore left him to roam about with his rifle. This was a glorious country for the youth; wild woods were all around him, and the game, having not yet learned to fear the crack of the rifle wandered fearlessly through them. This he thought was, of all places, the home for him. I hope you will not think that he was the idle and useless boy of the family, for it was not so. While the farm was improving, Daniel was supplying the family with provisions. The table at home was always filled with game, and they had enough and to spare. Their house became known as a warm-hearted and hospitable abode; for the wayfaring wanderer, when lost in the woods, was sure to find here a welcome, a shelter, and an abundance. Then, too, if money was wanted in the family, the peltries of the animals shot by Daniel supplied it: so that he was, in a large degree, the supporter of the household. In this way years rolled onward—the farm still enlarging and improving, Daniel still hunting, and the home one of constant peace, happiness, and plenty."

The industrious Daniel soon capitalized on his skills by starting a trade business, which required him to spend the fall through winter months in the woods and return in the spring with pelts and meat to trade for lead, powder, salt, and other goods the Boones needed. Thus began his lifelong habit of spending a great portion of his time away from home.

By 1754, the entire American border from Yadkin to the St. Lawrence River had become deeply concerned about hostile Native American activity. Though some settlers had established an uneasy peace with local tribes, others had mistakenly "put down stakes" on the centuries-old war path, placing them squarely in constant danger. (The "war path" served as a buffer zone between warring tribes and was frequently used as a highway.). Additionally, French and English interests had taken to stirring trouble for white settlers; forts were springing up across the landscape, drawing greater and greater attention to white encroachment on Native American lands.

Education

Like most pioneer children of the American frontier, Daniel had no actual "formal" schooling, relying on tutoring from family members to learn to read, write, and cipher (use numbers). "Subscription" schools, financed by the community at large to provide for the education of the children, had not yet become common. According to Boone family oral tradition, at age 14 Daniel's older brother's wife Sarah, said to have been far better educated than was common at this time, became Daniel's tutor and taught him to read, write and do arithmetic. Later in his life, Daniel kept journals of his survey work, using abilities assumed to have been self-taught, but his writing remained unorthodox.

A professional schoolteacher is said to have once expressed his concern over Daniel's lack of formal education, to which his father responded, "Let the girls do the spelling and Dan will do the shooting." But Boone historian John Mack Faragher has argued conversely that the folk image of Daniel portraying him as barely literate is likely fiction, and that Daniel "acquired a level of literacy that was the equal of most men of his times."[2] In fact, it seems Daniel was more literate than many of his contemporaries on the frontier. He would pack the Bible and *Gulliver's Travels* with him when he left on hunting expeditions, and he was often "the only literate person in groups of frontiersmen," sometimes entertaining his hunting companions by reading to them around the campfire.

Chapter 2: Military Man

French and Indian War

---

[2] Faragher, John Mack. *Daniel Boone: The Life and Legend of an American Pioneer.* Pages 16--17.

In 1755, British general Edward Braddock, commander-in-chief of the 13 colonies during the start of the French and Indian War (1754–1763), arrived in America intending to seize Fort Duquesne (now Pittsburgh) from the French. Joining the American militia was 20 year old Daniel Boone, who became one of several supply wagon drivers supporting the British effort to stop the advance of the French and their Native American allies through the Pennsylvania back country. Caught in a French Army-Native American ambush, Braddock chose to flee against superior numbers, with Daniel among the wagon drivers who escaped.

Though Daniel considered his war experience invaluable to the future of the burgeoning United States (and the family he was bound to protect), he found one aspect of his involvement much more enticing: that of meeting fellow longhunter, adventurer, and kindred spirit, John Finley. Finley had sparked Daniel's imagination for the "hunters' paradise" he'd visited in the western wilderness, a territory known as Kentucky, and upon his return home, Kentucky became a near-obsession for Daniel.

A year later, in 1756, Daniel married one of his neighbors, Rebecca Bryan. She too had a Quaker background and was said to be attractive and just as tall as the frontiersman himself. Over the course of the next 25 years, the couple would have 10 children, with all but two of them surviving to adulthood.

Except for Daniel's participation in British general Edward Braddock's failed attempt to seize Fort Duquesne from the French, the events of his life between 1755 and 1760 are for the most part speculation and urban legend. It is thought that at one point he hauled tobacco, may have served with the Rowan Rangers (under Baron William Henry Lyttelton), possibly helped defend Fort Dobbs (near Statesville, North Carolina) against hostile Cherokee, and may have served under General Hugh Waddell (leader of the North Carolina Provincial Militia). But all that is known with certainty is that he married in 1756, and sometime in 1760 during a hunting or scouting mission (or both) he may have carved a message on a tree trunk in eastern Tennessee, stating, "D Boon cilled a Bar on tree in the year 1760."[3] (*D. Boone killed a bear.*) Some historians are skeptical about the carvings, citing that Boone spelled his last name with the E at the end, and thus believe that the tree carvings are forgeries.

A year after his experience fighting the French and Indians in Pennsylvania, on August 14, 1756, Daniel married his sister-in-law Rebecca Ann "Becky" Bryan, the 17 year old daughter of neighbor Joseph Bryan, whose sister was married to his brother and was already a regular visitor to the Boone household. The ceremony was performed by his own father, Squire, who was by this time a Rowan County Justice of the Peace.

Described as a genuine pioneer woman "almost as handy with a rifle as her husband," their life

---

[3] Thwaites (Gold) Reuben, *Daniel Boone*. Page 56.

together was characterized by repeated moves as Daniel pushed deeper and deeper into the back country to maintain what he termed "elbow room," and live where game was most abundant. The couple would have nine children together: James, Israel, Susannah, Jemima, Lavinia, Rebecca, Daniel Morgan, John B., and Nathan (and by some accounts, ten).

Supporting his growing family as a "market hunter," Daniel's chosen profession (in addition to his various military responsibilities) made for long absences from home. Becky, whose chores included tending the garden, smoking bacon and venison, tending the dairy, looming cloth and making clothes, and even making moccasins was left to fend for herself and protect the children for long periods of time. Each autumn, Daniel would go on long hunts into the wilderness lasting weeks or even months with small groups of men who would amass hundreds of deer skins in the autumn and then trap beaver and otter through the winter. Returning in the spring, they would sell their take to commercial fur traders.

By 1764, Daniel had taken to bringing his seven- (or eight-) -year-old son James along on his travels—sometimes staying away from home as long as two or three months—with James thought to have been among the party who accompanied Daniel into central Florida in late 1765, when Daniel and several comrades explored the territory on horseback, considering it for settlement. And while Becky had became accustomed to pulling up stakes and moving deeper and deeper into the wilderness—where there was "neither law nor gospel"--following Daniel's return from Florida (where he'd staked a claim to property in Pensacola), she took her first stand, refusing to move to a "gameless land." Daniel ultimately agreed. A quote commonly attributed to Daniel during this time is what has been regarded as his description of the perfect ingredients to a happy life: "A good gun, a good horse, and a good wife."

By 1767, Daniel's travels had sparked a powerful desire to venture westward to the Kentucky Territory, a land said to be overflowing with wild game but also characterized as "dark and bloody ground" by whites who had traversed there. Venturing there first in the fall of that year as part of a hunting expedition led by longhunter and fellow explorer John Finley, Daniel found it everything he had ever heard or imagined: the richest farm land he had ever seen, salt springs thick with herds of buffalo, and woods teaming with deer and turkey.

In 1769, Daniel and several companions (including his brother-in-law John Stuart) set out for Kentucky on their own from North Carolina, following the "Warriors' Path", a well-worn but narrow trail used for centuries by Native Americans through the Cumberland Gap. In the 1768 Treaty of Fort Stanwix, the Iroquois had ceded their claim to Kentucky to the British. Ultimately remaining there for the next three years, he and his friends were twice robbed of their bounty by local Shawnee, with Daniel and John both captured but allowed to leave with the warning that if they ever again trespassed on tribal hunting-grounds, "wasps and yellow jackets will sting you severely."[4]

"Capture of Boone and Stuart" from Life and Times of Col. Daniel Boone by Cecil B. Hartley (1859)

Choosing to disregard the warning, Daniel decided to even the score by rustling Shawnee horses—only to be captured again. Managing to escape five days later, Daniel (now alone) chose to remain there for the next three months "without bread, salt, or sugar, without company of his fellow creatures, or even a horse or dog" in an attempt to recoup his loses.[5] At the verge of running out of ammunition, Daniel finally headed back home, with very little to show for his long stay away. For his own part, in 1770 Stuart would get separated from Daniel, and his remains would be found five years later, his cause of death only speculation.

Lord Dunmore's War (Conflict between Virginia Colony and the Shawnee and Mingo American Indian Nations, 1774)

Following the signing of the Treaty of Fort Stanwix, other Native tribes -- including the

---

[4] Thwaites (Gold) Reuben, *Daniel Boone*. Page 78.

[5] Thwaites (Gold) Reuben, *Daniel Boone*. Page 81.

Shawnee, who had not recognized the legitimacy of the treaty -- sought to send a message to whites planning to settle their lands. Native American hostilities on the Kentucky Territory frontier broke out with increasing frequency.

Daniel Boone would become a living legend in large measure due to the 1784 publication of *The Adventures of Colonel Daniel Boone*, which was authored by John Filson as part of his bigger work *The Discovery, Settlement And present State of Kentucke*. *The Adventures of Colonel Boone* were based off of personal interviews given by Boone, and it is factually detailed and far less embellished than the legends that would follow, but Filson still had to tidy up the wording. Though *The Adventures of Colonel Boone* reads as though it is being narrated by Boone himself, Filson adds rhetorical flourishes and makes it more readable.

In that famous account, *The Adventures of Colonel Boone* discusses just how fraught with danger the region was in 1769:

> "It was on the first of May, in the year 1769, that I resigned my domestic happiness for a time, and left my family and peaceable habitation on the Yadkin River, in North-Carolina, to wander through the wilderness of America, in quest of the country of Kentucke, in company with John Finley, John Stewart, Joseph Holden, James Monay, and William Cool. We proceeded successfully, and after a long and fatiguing journey through a mountainous wilderness, in a westward direction, on the seventh day of June following, we found ourselves on Red-River, where John Finley had formerly been trading with the Indians, and, from the top of an eminence, saw with pleasure the beautiful level of Kentucke. Here let me observe, that for some time we had experienced the most uncomfortable weather as a prelibation of our future sufferings. At this place we encamped, and made a shelter to defend us from the inclement season, and began to hunt and reconnoitre the country. We found every where abundance of wild beasts of all sorts, through this vast forest. The buffaloes were more frequent than I have seen cattle in the settlements, browzing on the leaves of the cane, or croping the herbage on those extensive plains, fearless, because ignorant, of the violence of man. Sometimes we saw hundreds in a drove, and the numbers about the salt springs were amazing. In this forest, the habitation of beasts of every kind natural to America, we practised hunting with great success until the twenty-second day of December following.
>
> This day John Stewart and I had a pleasing ramble, but fortune changed the scene in the close of it. We had passed through a great forest on which stood myriads of trees, some gay with blossoms, others rich with fruits. Nature was here a series of wonders, and a fund of delight. Here she displayed her ingenuity and industry in a variety of flowers and fruits, beautifully coloured, elegantly shaped, and charmingly flavoured;

and we were diverted with innumerable animals presenting themselves perpetually to our view.—In the decline of the day, near Kentucke river, as we ascended the brow of a small hill, a number of Indians rushed out of a thick cane-brake upon us, and made us prisoners. The time of our sorrow was now arrived, and the scene fully opened. The Indians plundered us of what we had, and kept us in confinement seven days, treating us with common savage usage. During this time we discovered no uneasiness or desire to escape, which made them less suspicious of us; but in the dead of night, as we lay in a thick cane-brake by a large fire, when sleep had locked up their senses, my situation not disposing me for rest, I touched my companion and gently awoke him. We improved this favourable opportunity, and departed, leaving them to take their rest, and speedily directed our course towards our old camp, but found it plundered, and the company dispersed and gone home. About this time my brother, Squire Boon, with another adventurer, who came to explore the country shortly after us, was wandering through the forest, determined to find me, if possible, and accidentally found our camp.

Notwithstanding the unfortunate circumstances of our company, and our dangerous situation, as surrounded with hostile savages, our meeting so fortunately in the wilderness made us reciprocally sensible of the utmost satisfaction. So much does friendship triumph over misfortune, that sorrows and sufferings vanish at the meeting not only of real friends, but of the most distant acquaintances, and substitutes happiness in their room. Soon after this, my companion in captivity, John Stewart, was killed by the savages, and the man that came with my brother returned home by himself. We were then in a dangerous, helpless situation, exposed daily to perils and death amongst savages and wild beasts, not a white man in the country but ourselves."

Undaunted by the unrest, on September 25, 1773 Boone packed up his family, and along with a number of his neighbors and some 50 British immigrants set out from North Carolina to establish a settlement in Kentucky. But even before reaching their destination, on October 9 Daniel's eldest son James and a small group of men who had left the main party to retrieve supplies were attacked by a band of Shawnees (by some accounts, joined by Delaware and Cherokee). James was ultimately tortured to death, and the brutality of the killings prompted Daniel's party to abandon the idea of settlement, sending shock waves along the frontier.

The following summer, Daniel volunteered to travel with a companion to Kentucky to notify surveyors in the area about the outbreak of hostilities. At least 20 other men bent on settling Kentucky were known to be surveying the countryside for settlement sites at this time. Traveling more than 800 miles in two months, Daniel and his companion rode settlement to settlement, camp to camp, warning those who had not already fled. Upon his return to southwest Virginia, Daniel then helped defend colonial settlements along the Clinch River, earning a promotion to captain in the militia, as well as the acclaim of his fellow citizens.

After the war, which was brief and ended after Virginia's victory at the Battle of Point Pleasant on October 10, 1774, the Shawnee relinquished their claims to Kentucky. But hostilities were far from over.

The American Revolutionary War

In 1775, North Carolina judge Richard Henderson formed the Transylvania Company, a partnership established to settle Kentucky. After buying a tract of land from the Cherokee, he hired Daniel Boone (who now commonly sported the fringed hunting shirt, deer-skin leggings and moccasins, and black felt hat he would become known for) to head a group of twenty-eight experienced woodsmen to blaze what would become known across the continent as the "Wilderness Road," interconnected pathways linking the "Warriors' Path" and other Native American trails leading to Kentucky and points west.

At the end of the Wilderness Road at a place known as "Boone's Trace" (just south of modern-day Lexington), Daniel and his men built a fort on the Kentucky River after surviving several attacks and prepared the way for three settlements: Boonesborough, Harrod's Town, and Benjamin Logan's. After building a new home for his family, Daniel then returned to South Carolina and in August of 1775 brought his wife and daughter Jemima to "Boonesborough," the first settlement completed in Transylvania. According to several historical documents, Harrodsburg was actually the first settlement, but pro-Boone historians claim it was not actually in Transylvania.

In American pioneering tradition, a settlement wasn't *permanent* until women arrived. As the first white women to see this part of the country, Becky and Jemima had to not only display a pioneering spirit few American women would even be called upon to exhibit but also learn to defend against frequent attacks from hostile neighboring Native American groups because Daniel was often hundreds of miles away.

The success of Judge Richard Henderson's Transylvania Company and plans for Kentucky was contingent on establishing Kentucky as America's Fourteenth Colony, but despite concerted efforts, Henderson lacked the political clout to obtain valid title to the lands. Thus, Kentucky was officially deemed a county of the State of Virginia and would not achieve statehood until 1792. As a result, Daniel and many other settlers would face land ownership issues for the next two decades.

As unexpected repercussion of the outbreak of the American Revolutionary War was increased violence in Kentucky as Native Americans, unhappy about the loss of Kentucky in treaties they didn't agree to, saw the War as a chance to drive out the colonists once and for all. Isolated settlers and hunters became the target of frequent attacks, convincing many potential settlers to abandon Kentucky. By late spring of 1776, fewer than two hundred colonists remained in Kentucky, residing primarily at the fortified settlements of Boonesborough, Harrodsburg, and Logan's Station.

On July 14, 1776, Daniel's daughter Jemima and two other teenage girls strayed too far from the settlement and were captured by a Shawnee war party, then spirited away towards Shawnee villages in the Ohio country. Following in quick pursuit, Daniel and a group of men from Boonesborough caught up with the band two days later, ambushed them while they stopped for a meal, and successfully rescued the girls. This incident would become the most celebrated and legendary event of Daniel's life, and as word spread of his bravery it helped make him one of the most famous men in America, but *The Adventures of Colonel Daniel Boone* offered a pretty muted account of the story:

> "On the fourteenth day of July, 1776, two of Col. Calaway's daughters, and one of mine, were taken prisoners near the fort. I immediately pursued the Indians, with only eight men, and on the sixteenth overtook them, killed two of the party, and recovered the girls. The same day on which this attempt was made, the Indians divided themselves into different parties, and attacked several forts, which were shortly before this time erected, doing a great deal of mischief. This was extremely distressing to the new settlers. The innocent husbandman was shot down, while busy cultivating the soil for his family's supply. Most of the cattle around the stations were destroyed. They continued their hostilities in this manner until the fifteenth of April, 1777, when they attacked Boonsborough with a party of above one hundred in number, killed one man, and wounded four—Their loss in this attack was not certainly known to us."

A 19th century illustration depicting the rescue of Jemima Boone and Betsey and Fanny

Callaway

In 1777, Henry Hamilton, the British Lieutenant Governor of Canada, began to recruit American Native American war parties to raid the three surviving settlements in Kentucky in an effort to seize control. On April 24 of that year, the Shawnee, led by Chief Blackfish, attacked Boonesborough. During the siege, Daniel was wounded in the leg by a bullet, which was said to have shattered his kneecap. While Daniel recovered, the Shawnees kept up their attacks around the settlement, killing the cattle and destroying crops. With the food supply running dangerously low, the settlers needed salt to preserve what meat they had left, so in January of 1778, Daniel led a party of thirty men to the springs on the Licking River to make salt and hopefully secure fresh meat.

Since first arriving in Kentucky ("Indian Territory"), Daniel had become the target of repeated attempted and successful capture, his apprehension becoming a mark of status for local chiefs. Their chance arrived when Daniel and the 30 other settlers set off to make salt and procure fresh meat for Boonesborough. Boone and the group were taken by surprise by a band of Shawnee warriors led by Chief Blackfish, who quickly captured all of them. Blackfish had planned to proceed directly to Boonesborough to capture its occupants, but Daniel convinced him that the women and children there were not hardy enough to survive a cross-country winter trek. Daniel promised Blackfish that if he would wait until spring, Boonesborough would surrender willingly without resistance. Unable to tell his men that it was only a ruse to stall for time, most were convinced he had switched loyalty to the British.

After first parading Daniel before various Shawnee villages north of the Ohio River and forcing him to endure the test of bravery known as "running the gauntlet", Chief Blackfish adopted Daniel as his son, the first white man to receive this distinction, but not before plucking all the hair from his head except the Shawnee-identifying "scalp lock" (a tuft of hair on the crown). The Shawnees also stripped him naked and washed his "white blood" away in a formal ceremony, and then painted him with red ochre.

Boone's ritual adoption by the Shawnees, from *Life & Times of Col. Daniel Boone*, by Cecil B. Hartley (1859)

The Adventures of Colonel Boone described his predicament:

"On the first day of January, 1778, I went with a party of thirty men to the Blue Licks, on Licking River, to make salt for the different garrisons in the country.

On the seventh day of February, as I was hunting, to procure meat for the company, I met with a party of one hundred and two Indians, and two Frenchmen, on their march against Boonsborough, that place being particularly the object of the enemy.

They pursued, and took me; and brought me on the eighth day to the Licks, where twenty-seven of my party were, three of them having previously returned home with the salt. I knowing it was impossible for them to escape, capitulated with the enemy, and, at a distance in their view, gave notice to my men of their situation, with orders not to resist, but surrender themselves captives.

The generous usage the Indians had promised before in my capitulation, was afterwards fully complied with, and we proceeded with them as prisoners to old Chelicothe, the principal Indian town, on Little Miami, where we arrived, after an uncomfortable journey, in very severe weather, on the eighteenth day of February, and received as good treatment as prisoners could expect from savages.—On the tenth day of March following, I, and ten of my men, were conducted by forty Indians to Detroit, where we arrived the thirtieth day, and were treated by Governor Hamilton, the British commander at that post, with great humanity.

During our travels, the Indians entertained me well; and their affection for me was so great, that they utterly refused to leave me there with the others, although the Governor offered them one hundred pounds Sterling for me, on purpose to give me a parole to go home. Several English gentlemen there, being sensible of my adverse fortune, and touched with human sympathy, generously offered a friendly supply for my wants, which I refused, with many thanks for their kindness; adding, that I never expected it would be in my power to recompense such unmerited generosity.

The Indians left my men in captivity with the British at Detroit, and on the tenth day of April brought me towards Old Chelicothe, where we arrived on the twenty-fifth day of the same month. This was a long and fatiguing march, through an exceeding fertile country, remarkable for fine springs and streams of water. At Chelicothe I spent my time as comfortably as I could expect; was adopted, accordin to their custom, into a family where I became a son, and had a great share in the affection of my new parents, brothers, sisters, and friends. I was exceedingly familiar and friendly with them, always appearing as chearful and satisfied as possible, and they put great confidence in me. I often went a hunting with them, and frequently gained their applause for my activity at our shooting-matches. I was careful not to exceed many of them in shooting; for no people are more envious than they in this sport. I could observe, in their countenances and gestures, the greatest expressions of joy when they exceeded me; and, when the reverse happened, of envy. The Shawanese king took great notice of me, and treated me with profound respect, and entire friendship, often entrusting me to hunt at my liberty. I frequently returned with the spoils of the woods, and as often presented some of what I had taken to him, expressive of duty to my sovereign. My food and lodging was, in common, with them, not so good indeed as I could desire, but necessity made every thing acceptable.

I now began to meditate an escape, and carefully avoided their suspicions, continuing with them at Old Chelicothe until the first day of June following, and then was taken by them to the salt springs on Sciotha, and kept there, making salt, ten days. During this time I hunted some for them, and found the land, for a great extent about this river, to exceed the soil of Kentucke, if possible, and remarkably well watered."

After living as a Shawnee for several months while many of his men had been traded or sold to other Shawnee tribes, on June 16, 1778 Daniel overheard that Blackfish was planning his return to Boonesborough with a large coalition of braves and British soldiers, so he executed a daring escape. Boone subsequently covered the 160 miles to Boonesborough in five days on horseback, and the last several miles on foot.

When Daniel arrived at the settlement, however, he discovered that not only had his wife and children (except for Jemima) returned to North Carolina on the assumption he was dead, but that many of the remaining men had serious doubts about Daniel's loyalty in light of the fact that for the past several months he had lived among the Shawnee. It also did not escape their notice that he looked the part thanks to the rituals performed on him. Daniel responded by organizing a preemptive raid against the Shawnee across the Ohio River and then returning to prepare a defense of the fort before Blackfish advanced.

While the boys (about 20 in number) stood guard around the perimeter of the settlement, the men (about 30 in number) reinforced the walls of the fort while the women prepared food and water and the children molded lead bullets. When Chief Blackfish arrived on September 7, 1778, his demand was simple: surrender or die.

The Adventures of Colonel Boone described the harrowing predicament the defenders found themselves in:

"I found our fortress in a bad state of defence, but we proceeded immediately to repair our flanks, strengthen our gates and posterns, and form double bastions, which we compleated in ten days. In this time we daily expected the arrival of the Indian army; and at length, one of my fellow prisoners, escaping from them, arrived, informing us that the enemy had an account of my departure, and postponed their expedition three weeks.—The Indians had spies out viewing our movements, and were greatly alarmed with our increase in number and fortifications. The Grand Councils of the nations were held frequently, and with more deliberation than usual. They evidently saw the approaching hour when the Long Knife would disposess them of their desirable habitations; and anxiously concerned for futurity, determined utterly to extirpate the whites out of Kentucke. We were not intimidated by their movements, but frequently gave them proofs of our courage.

About the first of August, I made an incursion into the Indian country, with a party of nineteen men, in order to surprise a small town up Sciotha, called Paint-Creek-Town. We advanced within four miles thereof, where we met a party of thirty Indians, on their march against Boonsborough, intending to join the others from Chelicothe. A smart fight ensued betwixt us for some time: At length the savages gave way, and fled. We had no loss on our side: The enemy had one killed, and two wounded. We took from them three horses, and all their baggage; and being informed, by two of our number that went to their town, that the Indians had entirely evacuated it, we proceeded no further, and returned with all possible expedition to assist our garrison against the other party. We passed by them on the sixth day, and on the seventh, we arrived safe at Boonsborough.

On the eighth, the Indian army arrived, being four hundred and forty-four in number, commanded by Capt. Duquesne, eleven other Frenchmen, and some of their own chiefs, and marched up within view of our fort, with British and French colours flying; and having sent a summons to me, in his Britannick Majesty's name, to surrender the fort, I requested two days consideration, which was granted.

It was now a critical period with us.—We were a small number in the garrison.—A powerful army before our walls, whose appearance proclaimed inevitable death, fearfully painted, and marking their footsteps with desolation. Death was preferable to captivity; and if taken by storm, we must inevitably be devoted to destruction. In this situation we concluded to maintain our garrison, if possible. We immediately proceeded to collect what we could of our horses, and other cattle, and bring them through the posterns into the fort: And in the evening of the ninth, I returned answer, that we were determined to defend our fort while a man was living—Now, said I to their commander, who stood attentively hearing my sentiments, We laugh at all your formidable preparations: But thank you for giving us notice and time to provide for our defence. Your efforts will not prevail; for our gates shall for ever deny you admittance.—Whether this answer affected their courage, or not, I cannot tell; but, contrary to our expectations, they formed a scheme to deceive us, declaring it was their orders, from Governor Hamilton, to take us captives, and not to destroy us; but if nine of us would come out, and treat with them, they would immediatly withdraw their forces from our walls, and return home peaceably. This sounded grateful in our ears; and we agreed to the proposal.

We held the treaty within sixty yards of the garrison, on purpose to divert them from a breach of honour, as we could not avoid suspicions of the savages. In this situation the articles were formally agreed to, and signed; and the Indians told us it was customary with them, on such occasions, for two Indians to shake hands with every white-man in the treaty, as an evidence of entire friendship. We agreed to this also, but were soon convinced their policy was to take us prisoners.—They immediately grappled us; but, although surrounded by hundreds of savages, we extricated ourselves from them, and escaped all safe into the garrison, except one that was wounded, through a heavy fire from their army. They immediately attacked us on every side, and a constant heavy fire ensued between us day and night for the space of nine days."

Having decided to hold out, Blackfish and a number of British soldiers would mount repeated assaults against the fort. After an initial failed attack, the Shawnee warriors began to tunnel beneath the walls of the fort, so Daniel assigned a detail to tunnel out to meet them. As night fell, Blackfish's men shot flaming arrows to ignite the thatched rooftops, so Daniel stationed a group of boys on the roofs to extinguish them. However, this forced the settlers to use most of their water supply to keep the fort from going up in flames, and when the Shawnee finally resorted to lighting brush to set the logs of the fortification on fire, the Boonesborough defenders seemed to be out of thought all hope — like their water had run out. But then "providence" stepped in. Suddenly it began to rain heavily, giving the defenders water, extinguishing the fires, and causing the tunnel to collapse. Despite having superior numbers, Chief Blackfish chose to withdraw and never threatened the fort again.

Following the attempted siege of Boonesborough, Captain Benjamin Logan and Colonel Richard Callaway, both of whom had nephews who were still Shawnee captives Daniel had "surrendered" to Blackfish, brought formal charges against Daniel for what they considered traitorous activities: the surrendering of his men and apparent defection to the Shawnee. Although ultimately found not guilty and even promoted to major after the court heard his testimony, Daniel was said to have been greatly humiliated by the court martial and the very idea that he would turn traitor to his family and friends. Afterward, he rarely spoke of it.

In the fall of 1779, Daniel returned to Kentucky with his family in tow, accompanied by a large party of immigrants (including, according to oral tradition, the family of Abraham Lincoln's grandfather). But rather than remain in Boonesborough, Daniel, seemingly always needing space when settlers became too numerous, founded the nearby settlement of Boone's Station.

With Transylvania land claims deemed invalidated after Virginia created and incorporated Kentucky County (meaning settlers needed to file new land claims with Virginia), Daniel began earning money as a land procurer, locating prime land for new arrivals. According to one enduring account, in 1780 Daniel collected nearly $20,000 in cash from various settlers, then set off to Williamsburg, Virginia to secure their land warrants. One night during the trip, however, the cash was stolen from his room while he was lodging in a tavern. Though some of the settlers forgave Daniel the loss, others insisted he repay the money, which took him several years to accomplish due to land-deed and financial issues of his own. While the land Daniel had surveyed (and claimed) had made him a rich man for a time, one of the richest in Kentucky in fact, he had to face the reality that he lacked the formal titles to claim ownership, thus resulting in legal claims against the very land he had cleared and built upon.

In 1780, Daniel joined General George Rogers Clark's invasion of the Ohio country and is thought to have fought at the Battle of Piqua on August 7. That November when Kentucky was divided into three Virginia counties, Daniel was promoted to lieutenant colonel in the Fayette County militia.

George Rogers Clark

In August of 1782, Lieutenant Colonel Daniel Boone fought at the Battle of Blue Licks, one of the last battles of the American Revolutionary War, during which his son Israel was killed. Boone accused his Native enemies of barbarity after the battle: "An exceeding fierce battle immediately began, for about fifteen minutes, when we, being over-powered by numbers, were obliged to retreat, with the loss of sixty-seven men; seven of whom were taken prisoners. The brave and much lamented Colonels Todd and Trigg, Major Harland and my second son, were among the dead. We were informed that the Indians, numbering their dead, found they had four killed more than we; and therefore, four of the prisoners they had taken, were, by general consent, ordered to be killed, in a most barbarous manner, by the young warriors, in order to train them up to cruelty; and then they proceeded to their towns."

In November of that year, Daniel participated in Brig. General George Roger Clark's expedition into Ohio to seize British-held Detroit, the last major campaign of the War. Cornwallis had surrendered at Yorktown in 1781, which is often considered the last major fighting of the Revolution, but as Boone's fighting indicates, the frontier was still a source of conflict, especially until the Treaty of Paris formally ended the war in 1783

Moreover, as the Revolutionary War was drawing to a close in November of 1783, the border war with Native American tribes north of the Ohio River escalated. In September 1786, Daniel took part in a military expedition into Ohio country led by Benjamin Logan, and although the Northwest Indian War (1785–1795) would continue until the American victory at the Battle of Fallen Timbers in 1794, the 1786 expedition was the last time Daniel would see military action.

When Virginia created Kanawha County in 1788, Daniel was appointed Lieutenant Colonel Boone of the Kanawha County Militia, but for all intents and purposes his fighting days were over.

Though he was a man of few words, Boone actually participated in politics beginning around the time the Revolution was drawing to a close. In April of 1781, Daniel Boone was elected as a representative to the Virginia General Assembly, held in Richmond, and the following year he was elected Sheriff of Fayette County, Virginia. In 1787, Daniel was again elected to the Virginia State Assembly, this time as a representative from Bourbon County, and in 1791 he was elected to the Virginia Legislature for the third time. Despite being elected several times, little is known about his political activities.

Chapter 3: Moving Around the Frontier

To say Daniel had just experienced a difficult decade would be an understatement, and that was a sentiment captured poignantly in *The Adventures of Colonel Daniel Boone*:

"I can now say that I have verified the saying of an old Indian who signed Col. Henderson's deed. Taking me by the hand, at the delivery thereof, Brother, says he, we have given you a fine land, but I believe you will have much trouble in settling it.—My footsteps have often been marked with blood, and therefore I can truly subscribe to its original name. Two darling sons, and a brother, have I lost by savage hands, which have also taken from me forty valuable horses, and abundance of cattle. Many dark and sleepless nights have I been a companion for owls, separated from the chearful society of men, scorched by the Summer's sun, and pinched by the Winter's cold, an instrument ordained to settle the wilderness. But now the scene is changed: Peace crowns the sylvan shade.

What thanks, what ardent and ceaseless thanks are due to that all-superintending Providence which has turned a cruel war into peace, brought order out of confusion, made the fierce savages placid, and turned away their hostile weapons from our country! May the same Almighty Goodness banish the accursed monster, war, from all lands, with her hated associates, rapine and insatiable ambition. Let peace, descending from her native heaven, bid her olives spring amidst the joyful nations; and plenty, in league with commerce, scatter blessings from her copious hand."

Of course, Daniel remained undeterred about life on the frontier. Around the end of the Revolutionary War, Daniel relocated to Limestone (renamed Maysville, Kentucky in 1786), which was then a booming Ohio River port. About a year later, he became something of a local celebrity around his 50th birthday when John Filson published *The Discovery, Settlement And present State of Kentucke*, which included a chronicle of Daniel's adventures.

While living in Maysville, Daniel kept a tavern and worked as a surveyor, horse trader, and land speculator. Though initially prosperous - he owned seven slaves by 1787, a relatively large number for Kentucky at a time when the land was dominated by small farms rather than large plantations - his prosperity did not last long.

After engaging in large-scale land speculation, Daniel finally became so frustrated with the legal hassles involved in land speculation by 1788 that he decided to move upriver to Point Pleasant, Virginia (now part of West Virginia). At Point Pleasant, he operated a trading post and occasionally worked as a surveyor's assistant. Though he successfully landed a contract to provide supplies to the Kanawha militia, his debts prevented him from buying goods on credit, so he closed his post and returned to what he enjoyed most, hunting and trapping.

In 1795, Daniel moved back to Kentucky, living in Nicholas County on land owned by his son Daniel Morgan Boone. According to a 1790 U. S. government census, 1,500 Kentucky settlers had been killed in Native American raids since the end of the Revolutionary War, but Daniel wanted to bring more people west, not send them back east. The following year, Daniel applied to Isaac Shelby, first governor of the new state of Kentucky, for a contract to widen the Wilderness Road into a wagon route, but the contract was awarded to someone else. Meanwhile, lawsuits over conflicting land claims continued to make their way through the Kentucky courts, with Daniel's remaining land claims sold off to pay legal fees and taxes—though he no longer paid strict attention to the process.

In 1798, a warrant was issued for Daniel's arrest after he ignored a summons to testify in a court case regarding land claims, but the sheriff apparently never actually endeavored to find him. In fact, that same year Kentucky named Boone County in his honor. Frustrated by all the legal problems, however, in 1799 Daniel followed his son Daniel Morgan to a frontier area that was then part of Spanish Louisiana (and eventually became the state of Missouri). He would spend the last two decades of his life there.

Chapter 4: Final Years

Intending to make a fresh start, Daniel moved with much of his extensive family to what is now St. Charles County, at which time the Spanish governor appointed him *syndic* (judge and jury) and commandant (military leader) of the *Femme Osage* District, positions he held until 1804. The many surviving anecdotes of Daniel's tenure as *syndic* suggest that he sought to render what he considered "fair" judgments rather than stick strictly to the letter of the law.

Boone lived much of the last part of his life with the family of his son Nathan in this home near present-day Defiance, Missouri

In 1804, the *Femme Osage* District became part of the U. S. Louisiana Territory included in the Louisiana Purchase, which encompassed 828,000 square miles of land formerly owned by France and comprised all or part of 15 current states and two Canadian provinces. Since Daniel's land grants from the Spanish government had been based on verbal agreements and handshakes, he once again lost all his land, forcing Daniel to petition Congress in 1809 to restore his Spanish land claims. They finally agreed to in 1814, but by then Daniel had been forced to sell most of this land to repay old Kentucky debts. According to legend, Daniel is said to have taken great pride in being able to travel back to Kentucky between 1810-1815 to finally pay off his outstanding debts, "leaving him with only fifty cents in his pocket." However, the Boone family has discounted any accounts of that trip.

With his wife Becky dying on March 18, 1813, the elderly Daniel spent his remaining years at the home of his son Daniel Morgan in St. Charles, Missouri, surrounded by his children and grandchildren, hunting and trapping as often as his failing health permitted. But even as Daniel's health began to fail him, the legendary tales about him did not. One incredible account claims that Daniel accompanied a group of hunters as far west as the Yellowstone River as late as 1810, at which point he would have been 75 years old.

Meanwhile, American painter John James Audubon claimed to have gone hunting with Daniel in the backwoods of Kentucky around 1810, and years later when he painted a portrait of Daniel he claimed to have done so from memory. However, skeptics have cast substantial doubt on Audubon's account, noting the similarity of this painting to the well-known portrait of Boone done by Chester Harding in 1820, shortly before his death. Moreover, the Boone family insists that Daniel never returned to Kentucky after 1799, though some historians have disputed that assertion and note Boone might have visited his brother Squire in Kentucky in 1810. If so, that would give Audubon's story potential authenticity.

Another unlikely account of Boone's frontier travels credits him with traveling to Fort Osage, Missouri in 1816, when he would have been over 80. Nevertheless, an officer at the Fort claimed, "We have been honored by a visit from Colonel Boon, the first settler of Kentucky; he lately spent two weeks with us…He left this for the river Platt, some distance above. Col Boon is eighty-five years of age, five feet seven inches high, stoutly made, and active for one of his years; is still of vigorous mind, and is pretty well informed. He has taken part in all the wars of America, from before Braddock's war to the present hour."

In 1820, Chester Harding painted the only known contemporary portrait of Daniel Boone, and since he was probably the only artist to paint Daniel in his lifetime, other depictions of Boone (including Audubon's) were adapted from his work. Painted just three or four months before his death, it is said that Daniel was so frail that he had to be steadied by a friend while the artist worked. From the original oil sketch, Harding went on to produce two more busts and a full-length portrait.

Daniel Boone died of natural causes on September 26, 1820 just a few weeks shy of his 86th birthday while visiting his son Nathan on *Femme Osage* Creek. Legend claims that his dying words were, "I'm going now. My time has come."[6] He was buried next to his wife Becky, who had died seven years earlier, and his obituary in a Missouri newspaper read, "At the age of eighty, in company with one white man and a black man, whom he laid under strict injunction to return him to his family dead or alive, he made a hunting trip to the headwaters of the Great Osage, where he was successful in trapping of beaver, and in taking other game." As might be expected, and somewhat fittingly, the newspaper's account of Boone's life was full of erroneous details and riddled with inaccuracies.

Upon his death, the Constitutional Convention of Missouri went into a 20 day period of mourning.

Homage

---

[6] Gordy, Wilbur F. Daniel Boone, the Kentucky Pioneer."

1861 engraving depicting an elderly Boone

The log cabin Squire and Sarah Boone built in 1731 is partially preserved today as the "Daniel Boone Homestead."

On July 14, 1776, Daniel's daughter Jemima and two other teenage girls were captured outside Boonesborough by a Shawnee war party and carried north towards the Ohio country. Following a dramatic race across the countryside and subsequent ambush, Daniel and his men successfully rescued the girls—an event that became the most celebrated and legendary event of Daniel Boone's life. In 1826, James Fenimore Cooper fictionalized the event in his classic book, *The Last of the Mohicans*.

In 1845 the remains of Daniel and Becky Boone were moved to Kentucky to rest in the renowned pioneer's "hunter's paradise," with a monument placed there in his memory. There is ongoing controversy, however, regarding the final disposition of Daniel's remains, with some insisting that the wrong remains were removed and re-buried (thus, Daniel and Rebecca are still buried in Missouri), while others (unhappy they were removed) demand the return of the bodies to Missouri.

Between 1851 and 1852, Missouri artist George Caleb Bingham painted *Daniel Boone Escorting Settlers through the Cumberland Gap,* which became one of the most popular American paintings addressing the theme of westward expansion. Rich in symbolism, it helped establish the mythic status of Daniel Boone and legends of western settlement.

In 1853, German painter Charles Wimar painted *The Abduction of Daniel Boone's Daughter by the Indians,* a painting which draws from Christian and classical imagery to justify and romanticize westward expansion and the underlying ideal of "Manifest Destiny."

In 1915, the marking of the Boone Trail through North Carolina, Virginia, Tennessee, and Kentucky was completed (ending at Boonesborough), with the first marker set at Daniel's early home on the Yadkin River.

Today, the only remnant of the original settlement at Boonesborough is a graveyard.

Among the many geographic locations named for Daniel Boone are Daniel Boone National Forest, the Sheltowee Trace Trail, the town of Boone, North Carolina, and seven American counties: Boone County, Illinois, Boone County, Indiana, Boone County, Nebraska, Boone County, West Virginia, Boone County, Missouri, Boone County, Kentucky, and Boone County, Arkansas.

A number of schools across the nation are also named for Daniel Boone including those located in Birdsboro, Pennsylvania, Douglassville, Pennsylvania, Gray, Tennessee, and Chicago, Illinois.

Additionally, the U. S. Navy's James Madison-class Polaris submarine, the USS *Daniel Boone*, was named for Daniel.

Daniel's name has long been synonymous with the American outdoors prompting the formation of the *Boone and Crockett Club* (a conservationist organization founded by Theodore Roosevelt in 1887), and the *Sons of Daniel Boone*, which was the previous incarnation of the *Boy Scouts of America*.

On the bicentennial of Boone's birth, the Daniel Boone half dollar was issued by the federal government as a commemorative coin.

Chapter 5: Boone's Legacy

Perspective

For over two centuries, historians, poets, and romance writers have sang the praises of Daniel Boone and credited him with founding Kentucky and establishing the first settlement there. In reality, Daniel was neither the founder of Kentucky (he was led there himself by fellow longhunter John Finley) nor did he establish the first settlement (state documents show that Harrodsburg preceded Boonsborough by at least a year).

While he might not have been the first, that's not to say that Daniel wasn't instrumental in settling Kentucky and in helping establish a level of peace that made it inhabitable. And he almost certainly was a great hunter, insatiable explorer, capable surveyor, and natural land-pilot. But in the larger scheme of American pioneer history, he can't compare with men like Virginian George Rogers Clark or Benjamin Logan. Though Boone is credited with "civilizing" the frontier, that was if anything more a product of his constant desire to find what he termed "elbow room."[7]

Frontiersman, Trailblazer, Defender

During Daniel Boone's lifetime, America evolved from a group of colonies with fewer than a million inhabitants clustered along the Atlantic Seaboard to an independent nation of close to ten million reaching well beyond the Mississippi River. This was made possible by trails west.

---
[7] Thwaites (Gold) Reuben, *Daniel Boone*. Page viii.

More than any other man of his time, Daniel Boone is credited with blazing trails through the Cumberland Gap (a notch in the Appalachian Mountains located near the intersection of Kentucky, Virginia and Tennessee), through the interior of Kentucky, and on to the Ohio River Valley. A trail known as the "Wilderness Road," it served as the main access route to western United States for some 300,000 families over the course of 35 years. And though he didn't accomplish this feat alone, it was Daniel's leadership in establishing and defending the settlement of Boonesborough (and others) that enabled white settlers to hold their ground and not have to flee the frontier along Kentucky during the Revolution. This would ultimately ensure Kentucky's admission to the Union as the 15th state in 1792.

In times of strife, which aptly described day-to-day life in frontier Kentucky, people gravitated towards Daniel and relied on his unique experience, particularly his knowledge of "Indian" tactics and "ways of the wilderness." Though border warfare between settlers and Native Americans made for long periods of desperation during which settlers feared for their very existence, Daniel always led by example, never becoming callous about killing and always advocating the avoidance of bloodshed whenever possible. While it's clear that when his raised his arms in defense of his family, friends, or others in need, he became a deadly foe, he was never known to boast of killing, as made clear by the understated account of his actions in *The Adventures of Colonel Boone*.

Like other frontier settlers of the era, there is little doubt that Daniel Boone had a fundamental hatred of Native Americans, viewing them as competitors for the same ground and a threat to his family. To him, it was simply a matter of which side would ultimately dominate what he considered open lands. Although the former Quaker had been reared to share the land and live in harmony, when he no longer believed that was possible Boone used his considerable survival skills to stake his claim.

Man and Myth

"I can't say as ever I was lost, but I was bewildered once for three days." – Daniel Boone

In Print

Daniel Boone's great adventures became well known in the 18th century through what was then considered an "autobiographical account," John Filson's "The Adventures of Colonel Daniel Boon," part of his *Discovery, Settlement, and Present State of Kentucke* (published in 1784). Cecil B. Hartley's *Life & Times of Col. Daniel Boone* is another attempt at an objective biography that, while not entirely without embellishment, presents Boone in a biographical light short of the outright tall tales that would become the stuff of television and theater.

The Daniel Boone that everyone knows today was made by the stories of Boone that followed in such popular accounts like Francis L. Hawks' *The Adventures of Daniel Boone: the Kentucky rifleman*. Boone was transformed from scrappy frontiersman to the embodiment of a folk hero. Daniel's myth was further perpetuated in Lord Byron's homage in *Don Juan* (published in 1837), which gave the name Daniel Boone even more international renown. Much of Daniel Boone's life was also covered by William Henry Bogart in his book, *Daniel Boone and the Hunters of Kentucky*, published in 1930.

Perhaps the biggest addition to the Boone legend came from author Timothy Flint. Like John Filson, Flint also claimed to have interviewed Daniel Boone for his *Biographical Memoir of Daniel Boone, the First Settler of Kentucky*. Published in 1833, it eventually became one of the best-selling biographies of the 19th century. However, historians note that Flint greatly embellished Daniel's adventures, doing for Boone what Parson Weems did for George Washington. In Flint's book, Daniel fights hand-to-hand with a bear, escapes from a band of hostile Native Americans by swinging on vines ala Tarzan, and displays near superhuman feats of endurance.

Although the Boone family is said to have thought the book absurd, Flint greatly influenced the popular image of Daniel Boone, with his "reenactments" appearing in countless "dime" novels and books aimed at young boys, for decades to follow. Daniel Boone comic books were still quite popular among American youth well into the 1960s, when they were replaced by *Superman* and other superheroes. At least three well-known American entertainers have claimed kinship with Daniel Boone: actor and singer Pat Boone, Richard Boone of the TV series *Have Gun, Will Travel,* and Randy Boone from the classic Western series, *The Virginian*.

Though historical scholarship has disproved many of the legends and deeds attributed to Daniel Boone, historians rarely discredit the qualities of courage and determination that earned Daniel enduring popularity and folk-hero status. While every account of Boone should be read with a proverbial *grain of salt*, they continue to feed the frontiersman image and keep Daniel Boone's memory larger-than-life.

Unlike so many others, Boone's status as a frontier folk hero was not helped by self-promotion. Boone was not as widely-known for storytelling as fellow frontiersman Davy Crockett, who spun his own yarns and tall tales around campfires. But historian and biographer Reuben Goldthwaites described Daniel as a man fond of singing who sometimes "sang merrily at the top of his voice," and gladly spent hours "relating tales of stirring adventures."[8] Some historians speculate that Daniel may have followed the madrigal tradition of putting stories or verse to tune.

---

[8] Thwaites (Gold) Reuben, *Daniel Boone*. Page 94.

Daniel Boone in Pop Culture

"Daniel Boone was a man,
Yes, a big man!
With an eye like an eagle
And as tall as a mountain was he!
Daniel Boone was a man,
Yes, a big man!
He was brave, he was fearless
And as tough as a mighty oak tree!" – Lyrics of the theme song for the television series *Daniel Boone* (1964-1970).

Boone emerged into American popular culture as a living legend largely due to John Filson's *The Discovery, Settlement And present State of Kentucke*. When that work was quickly translated into French and German, it made the name Daniel Boone famous in America and Europe as synonymous with pioneering. Boone's adventures, actual and mythologized, formed the basis of the archetypal hero of the American West popular in 19th-century novels. For example, the protagonist of James Fenimore Cooper's *Leatherstocking Tales*, the first of which was published in 1823, bore striking similarities to Daniel. Even the protagonist's name, Nathaniel Bumppo, was a derivative of Boone's. In keeping with this theme, *The Last of the Mohicans*, Cooper's second *Leatherstocking* novel (published in 1826), featured a fictionalized version of Daniel's famed rescue of his daughter from the Shawnee.

Throughout the 20th century, Daniel Boone was featured in numerous American comic strips and radio programs, where the emphasis was usually on action and melodrama rather than historical accuracy, much to readers' and listeners' delight. Since 1957, the play "Horn in the West," a fictionalized account of the lives of settlers whom Daniel Boone led into the Appalachian Mountains, has been performed annually in Boone, North Carolina.

By the 20th century, the legends of Boone were both so outlandish and ingrained in memory that many Americans started to believe he was actually a fictional character. In 1936, *Daniel Boone*, an American film directed by David Howard with George O'Brian in the title role, was shown in American theaters, presented with the promo, "In 1775, Daniel Boone leads thirty colonial families to Kentucky where they face two threats: Native American raiders led by renegade white Simon Girty, who opposes the colony; and the schemes of effete Stephen Marlowe to seize title to the new lands. Perils, battles, escapes, and a love interest round out the film."

Boone came back to life for these audiences with NBC's *Daniel Boone* television series, aired from 1964 to 1970 with Fess Parker in the title role. Parker was previously associated with frontier heroes by playing Davy Crockett in a series presented by Walt Disney in their "anthology television series." Country-Western singer-actor Jimmy Dean portrayed Josh Clements during the 1968–1970 seasons of the show, with actor and former NFL football player Rosey Grier making regular appearances as Gabe Cooper in the 1969-1970 season.

Enlivened in part by the popular TV series theme song, Daniel was described as a "big man" in a "coonskin cap," and the "rippin'est, roarin'est, fightin'est man the frontier ever knew!" Though historically inaccurate -- Daniel Boone was not a big man and wore a felt hat rather than a coonskin cap — viewers made the series and the image quite popular, even as critics of the time noted that Parker was essentially reprising his role as Davy Crockett from the earlier TV series. Another TV treatment of the life of Daniel Boone appeared in 1960 as part of the *"Disney anthology series"* with Dewey Martin in the title role, but had far less public appeal than Fess Parker's Daniel Boone, most likely because he was already identifiable with the buckskin-wearing persona.

All of this may have illustrated just how little the American public actually knew about the historic Daniel Boone, something that could still be said today, but it also proves just how enduring and popular Boone's legacy has become and remains.

Bibliography

Bakeless, John. *Daniel Boone: Master of the Wilderness*. Nebraska: University of Nebraska Press, 1989.

Daugherty, James H. *Daniel Boone*. New York: Viking Books, 1967.

Elliott, Lawrence. *The Long Hunter: A New Life of Daniel Boone*. New York: Reader's Digest Press, 1976.

Faragher, John Mack. *Daniel Boone: The Life and Legend of an American Pioneer*. New York: Holt, 1992.

Gordy, Wilbur F. 泥aniel Boone, the Kentucky Pioneer • (1903). Accessed via http://www.legendsofamerica.com/ah-danielboone.html 09.12.2012.

Thwaites (Gold) Reuben, *Daniel Boone*. New York: D. Appleton & Company, 1903. Accessed via http://archive.org/stream/danielboone01thwa#page/n9/mode/2up 09.11.2012.

Wisconsin Historical Archives website, Personal Papers of Daniel Boone at the Wisconsin Historical Society, accessed via http://arcat.library.wisc.edu/ 09.09.2012.

Davy Crockett and Jim Bowie

The Fall of the Alamo by Robert Jenkins Onderdonk depicts Davy Crockett swinging his rifle at Mexican troops who have breached the south gate of the mission.

Chapter 1: Crockett's Early Years

A replica log cabin built on the site of Crockett's birth

"AS THE public seem to feel some interest in the history of an individual so humble as I am, and as that history can be so well known to no person living as to myself, I have, after so long a time, and under many pressing solicitations from my friends and acquaintances, at last determined to put my own hand to it, and lay before the world a narrative on which they may at least rely as being true. And seeking no ornament or colouring for a plain, simple tale of truth, I throw aside all hypocritical and fawning apologies, and, according to my own maxim, just "go ahead." – *Narrative of the Life of David Crockett of the State of Tennessee*

The Crockett Family Tree

David "Davy" Crockett was born on August 17, 1786 in a pioneer cabin in eastern Tennessee in what is now Greene County, Tennessee, close to the Nolichucky River (near the community of Lime Stone), the fifth son of nine children born to John and Rebecca Hawkins Crockett. Among his siblings were older brothers Nathan, William, Aaron, and James Patterson; younger brother John; and sisters Margaret Catharine, Elizabeth ("Betsy"), and Rebecca. Prior to the time John and Rebecca married, John was a farmer living in Pennsylvania and then North Carolina; Rebecca, an American-born woman from Maryland.

Of Irish, English, Scottish, and French-Huguenot ancestry, the Crockett family name (also Crocket, Croket, Crocit, and Crokit) can be traced to Monsieur de la Croquetagne, a captain in the Royal Guard of French King Louis XIV (September 1638--September 1715). Having converted to Protestantism, as Huguenots (members of the Protestant Reformed Church of France) the Crockett family was forced to flee religious persecution in 17th century France, settling in Ireland.

Crockett family oral tradition claims that David's father was born on the voyage to America from Ireland, though documents indicate that David's great-grandfather, William David Crockett, is registered as having been born in New Rochelle, New York in 1709. Even Davy was not sure which account is accurate, as he noted in the autobiographical *Narrative of the Life of David Crockett of the State of Tennessee*. David's father John, one of the well-known "Over-mountain Men," fought against British and Tory forces at the Battle of Kings Mountain (October 7, 1780, south of present-day Kings Mountain, North Carolina) during the American Revolutionary War.

David, who for most of his life was known as "Davy", is said to have been named after his paternal grandfather, William David Crockett, who along with his wife was killed in 1777 at his home near present-day Rogersville, Tennessee, during a raid by Creek and Cherokee Native Americans led by Chief Dragging Canoe. Davy wrote of an uncle who was also captured by Native Americans in his autobiography, "At the same time, the Indians wounded Joseph Crockett, a brother to my father, by a ball, which broke his arm; and took James a prisoner, who was still a younger brother than Joseph, and who, from natural defects, was less able to make his escape, as he was both deaf and dumb. He remained with them for seventeen years and nine months, when he was discovered and recollected by my father and his eldest brother, William Crockett; and was purchased by them from an Indian trader, at a price which I do not now remember; but so it was, that he was delivered up to them, and they returned him to his relatives."

The Tennessee Frontier

Davy Crockett's life, legend, and autobiography were all built upon the same foundation of colorful frontier stories. While there's no doubt Davy was a frontier boy through and through, it's hard to determine how much embellishment he added to his stories. Legend contends that Davy became a crack shot with a longrifle at a very early age due to fear of being punished for wasting shot, and even as a child, Crockett speaks of two episodes in glaring detail during his very early years:

> "Just a little distance below them, there was a fall in the river, which went slap-right straight down. My brothers, though they were little fellows, had been used to paddling the canoe, and could have carried it safely anywhere about there; but this fellow Campbell wouldn't let them have the paddle, but, fool like, undertook to manage it

himself. I reckon he had never seen a water craft before; and it went just any way but the way he wanted it. There he paddled, and paddled, and paddled—all the while going wrong,—until,—in a short time, here they were all going, straight forward, stern foremost, right plump to the falls; and if they had only had a fair shake, they would have gone over as slick as a whistle. It was'ent this, though, that scared me; for I was so infernal mad that they had left me on the shore, that I had as soon have seen them all go over the falls a bit, as any other way. But their danger was seen by a man by the name of Kendall, but I'll be shot if it was Amos; for I believe I would know him yet if I was to see him. This man Kendall was working in a field on the bank, and knowing there was no time to lose, he started full tilt, and here he come like a cane brake afire; and as he ran, he threw off his coat, and then his jacket, and then his shirt, for I know when he got to the water he had nothing on but his breeches. But seeing him in such a hurry, and tearing off his clothes as he went, I had no doubt but that the devil or something else was after him—and close on him, too—as he was running within an inch of his life. This alarmed me, and I screamed out like a young painter. But Kendall didn't stop for this. He went ahead with all might, and as full bent on saving the boys, as Amos was on moving the deposites. When he came to the water he plunged in, and where it was too deep to wade he would swim, and where it was shallow enough he went bolting on; and by such exertion as I never saw at any other time in my life, he reached the canoe, when it was within twenty or thirty feet of the falls; and so great was the suck, and so swift the current, that poor Kendall had a hard time of it to stop them at last, as Amos will to stop the mouths of the people about his stockjobbing. But he hung on to the canoe, till he got it stop'd, and then draw'd it out of danger. When they got out, I found the boys were more scared than I had been, and the only thing that comforted me was, the belief that it was a punishment on them for leaving me on shore.

Shortly after this, my father removed, and settled in the same county, about ten miles above Greenville.

There another circumstance happened, which made a lasting impression on my memory, though I was but a small child. Joseph Hawkins, who was a brother to my mother, was in the woods hunting for deer. He was passing near a thicket of brush, in which one of our neighbours was gathering some grapes, as it was in the fall of the year, and the grape season. The body of the man was hid by the brush, and it was only as he would raise his hand to pull the bunches, that any part of him could be seen. It was a likely place for deer; and my uncle, having no suspicion that it was any human being, but supposing the raising of the hand to be the occasional twitch of a deer's ear, fired at the lump, and as the devil would have it, unfortunately shot the man through the body. I saw my father draw a silk handkerchief through the bullet hole, and entirely through his body; yet after a while he got well, as little as any one would have thought it. What become of him, or whether he is dead or alive, I don't know; but I reckon he did'ent fancy the business of gathering grapes in an out-of-the-way thicket soon again."

In 1792, following numerous failed business ventures and a flood that washed away the Crockett home, John moved his family to a one-room log cabin on a one hundred ninety-seven-acre tract of land near Morristown, Tennessee, in the Southwest Territory. While Davy remembers the move as having been prompted by his mother Rebecca's desire to live near her brother Joseph, historians think it just as likely that the Crockett family was simply staying one step ahead of debt collectors.

By November of 1795, John, who had slowly been selling off his land to pay his debts, was forced to auction off his last few remaining parcels. Moving then to a tract of land owned by a Quaker settler named John Canaday, John built and operated a tavern on the Knoxville, Tennessee - Abingdon, Virginia travel route, which Davy described as "on the small scale, as he [John] was poor; and the principal accommodations he kept were for the waggoners [sic] who traveled the road."[9] The tavern also served as the Crockett family home. Among Davy's daily chores were seeing to the travelers' comfort needs and supplying fresh meat for the supper table.

In his 1834 autobiography, *A Narrative of the Life of David Crockett* (also appearing as *The Autobiography of David Crockett*), Davy describes his early life as filled with adventure, hardship, and travel. And as was common practice on the eighteenth-century Tennessee frontier, for several years beginning in 1798, hardship came in the form of being hired-out ("binded") by his father to more prosperous farmers. A man of consistently little means, John thought it of greater value to the family for Davy to work neighboring farms than their own meager plot. And in that in the Crockett household anyone who did not work "was not worth their keep," even Davy's elder sister Margaret Catharine was bound out, as John was perpetually in debt.

Binding

One often-told account describes a twelve-year-old Davy hired out to a cattle drover named Siler, from whom he ultimately had to escape after he convinced Davy to remain with him past the end of his contract. As Davy described it:

"An old Dutchman, by the name of Jacob Siler, who was moving from Knox County to Rockbridge, in the state of Virginia, in passing, made a stop at my father's house. He had a large stock of cattle, that he was carrying on with him; and I suppose made some proposition to my father to hire some one to assist him. Being hard run every way . . . and as little as I knew about travelling [sic] or being from home, he hired me to the old Dutchman, to go four hundred miles on foot, with a perfect stranger that I never had

---

[9] Wallis, Michael. *David Crockett: The Lion of the West.* Page 43.

seen until the evening before.

> I set out with a heavy heart, it is true, but I went ahead, until we arrived at the place, which was three miles from what is called the Natural Bridge . . . My Dutch master was very kind to me, and gave me five or six dollars, being pleased, as he said, with my services . . . [But then] he persuaded me to stay with him, and not return any more to my father. I had been taught so many lessons of obedience by my father, that I at first supposed I was bound to obey this man, or at least I was afraid openly to disobey him; and I therefore staid with him."

Finally deciding to sneak away, Davy was forced to make his way home across the wilderness through eight inches of snow, or so the story goes.

Start of the Adventure

In Davy's own words, "As my father was very poor, and living as he did far back in the back woods, he had neither the means nor the opportunity to give me, or any of the rest of his children, any learning."[10] Even so, it appears that in 1799, at the age of thirteen, he and his four older brothers were sent to Benjamin Kitchen's country subscription school at nearby Barton Springs, where a community-paid teacher offered classes in the "Three Rs": reading, [w]riting, and 'rithmetic. By some accounts, Davy had received over three-months' tutoring at the home of a "book learned" neighbor prior to this time. But it took all of four days for Davy to drop out, deciding it better to run away from home than suffer imminent punishment for the serious indiscretion he'd committed:

> "I went four days, and had just began to learn my letters a little, when I had an unfortunate falling out with one of the scholars,—a boy much larger and older than myself. I knew well enough that though the school-house might do for a still hunt, it wouldn't do for a drive, and so I concluded to wait until I could get him out, and then I was determined to give him salt and vinegar. I waited till in the evening, and when the larger scholars were spelling, I slip'd out, and going some distance along his road, I lay by the way-side in the bushes, waiting for him to come along. After a while he and his company came on sure enough,[30] and I pitched out from the bushes and set on him like a wild cat. I scratched his face all to a flitter jig, and soon made him cry out for quarters in good earnest. The fight being over, I went on home, and the next morning was started again to school; but do you think I went? No, indeed. I was very clear of it; for I expected the master would lick me up, as bad as I had the boy. So, instead of going to the school-house, I laid out in the woods all day until in the evening the scholars were dismissed, and my brothers, who were also going to school, came along,

[10] Project Gutenberg eBook, "A Narrative of the Life of David Crockett, of the State of Tennessee, by Davy Crockett." [16].

returning home. I wanted to conceal this whole business from my father, and I therefore persuaded them not to tell on me, which they agreed to."

The next morning, fearful that word of the ambush would lead to repercussions from his teacher, friends of the bully, and certainly, from his father, Davy ran away--ending up at the home of Jesse Creek, owner of a general store just a few miles away. Cheek immediately hired Davy as a drover to accompany him on a cattle drive bound for Virginia.

Though intended as a short cooling-off period allowing his misdeed to be forgotten, and his father to forgive him for dropping out of classes after less than a week (at a considerable expense), Davy would spend nearly three years traveling town to town. By the time he finally returned home in the spring of 1802, his father, who'd long before forgiven Davy, had assumed his son most likely dead.

Prodigal Son

According to legend (and Davy's *Narrative*), Davy Crockett ran away from home in 1799 at age thirteen following that fight in school and spent nearly three years roaming from town to town as a cattle drover, honing the skills of an outdoorsman, hunter, and trapper. Of course, this account may very well have been a later fabrication designed to illustrate his sense of independence and inherent frontier survival skills.

In 1802, several months short of his 16th birthday, Davy is said to have returned home after nearly three years roaming the countryside, arriving at his parents' tavern unannounced. Having had "no thought or expectation . . . for they had long given [Davy] up for lost," it was only after he'd checked in as a guest and joined the others at the supper table that he was recognized, his sister grabbing him around the neck and exclaiming, "Here is my lost brother!"[11] Presumably, it was at this time that Davy began his lifelong habit of regaling family and friends with tales of his fantastic exploits and adventures.

Though his family was delighted that he was once again in their midst, his father John soon convinced Davy to hire out to one Abraham Wilson to settle a debt of $36 (an arrangement requiring six-months' labor), and then John Canaday (owner of the property on which the Crockett tavern set) to work off a $40 debt. Once this obligation was settled, Davy continued to work for Canaday for himself.

Marriage

"I found a family of very pretty little girls that I had known when very young. They had lived in the same neighborhood with me, and I had thought very well of them. I

---
[11] Wallis, Michael. *David Crockett: The Lion of the West*. Page 57.

made an offer to one of them, whose name is nobody's business, no more than the Quaker girl's was, and I found she took it very well. I still continued paying my respects to her, until I got to love her as bad as I had the Quaker's niece; and I would have agreed to fight a whole regiment of wild cats if she would only have said she would have me. Several months passed in this way, during all of which time she continued very kind and friendly. At last, the son of the old Quaker and my first girl had concluded to bring their matter to a close, and my little queen and myself were called on to wait on them. We went on the day, and performed our duty as attendants. This made me worse than ever; and after it was over, I pressed my claim very hard on her, but she would still give me a sort of an evasive answer. However, I gave her mighty little peace, till she told me at last she would have me. I thought this was glorification enough, even without spectacles. I was then about eighteen years old. We fixed the time to be married; and I thought if that day come, I should be the happiest man in the created world, or in the moon, or any where else."

In 1805, 19 year old Davy proposed to Margaret Elder, a young woman Davy describes as "a tall, buxom lass with cherry bitten cheeks and luscious lips, mischievous eyes, and hands doubly accustomed to handing the spinning wheel or rifle trigger". However, Margaret ultimately jilted him, opting to marry someone else, even though the drawn up marriage contract, dated October 21, 1805, has been preserved by the courthouse in Dandrige, Tennessee.[12] Davy is said to have concluded, "[I'm] only born for hardships, misery, and disappointment."[13]

---

[12] Wallis, Michael. *David Crockett: The Lion of the West*. Page 68.

[13] Wallis, Michael. *David Crockett: The Lion of the West*. Page 70.

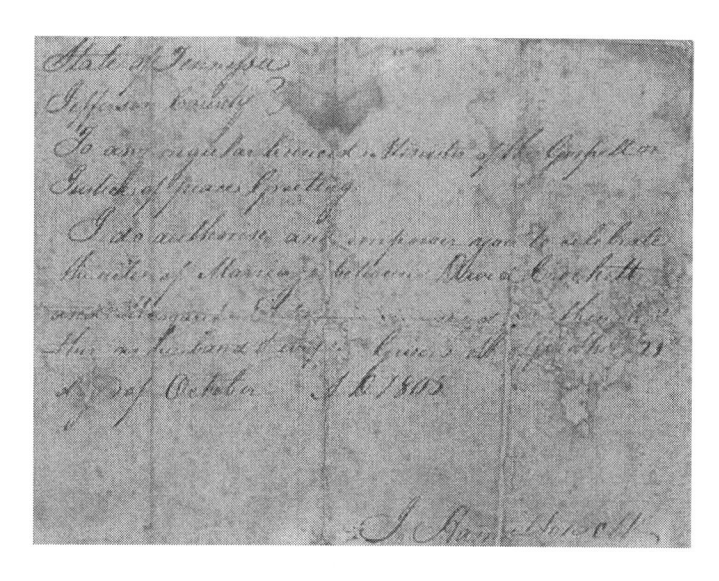

Crockett's marriage contract

The following year, Davy encountered Mrs. Jean Finley, wife of William Finley, a mother of eight who upon meeting the rebounding Davy told him that she had the perfect sweetheart for him: her daughter Mary (who went by her middle name, Polly). Upon meeting the eldest daughter, Davy affirmed being "well pleased with her from the word go. She had a good countenance, and was very pretty, and I was full bent on making up an acquaintance with her."[14]

On August 16, 1806, one day before his 20th birthday, Davy married Mary Polly Finley in Jefferson County, Tennessee. They would have two sons together: John Wesley (born July 10, 1807) and William Finley (born November 25, 1809). The boys were followed on November 25, 1812 by daughter Margaret, who also came to be known as "Polly."

As wild game became increasingly scarce in their part of Tennessee, in 1813 Davy moved his family to Franklin County, Tennessee, naming the new settlement on Beans Creek "Kentuck." Early in 1815, Davy's wife died. Historians speculate that she was afflicted by one of several common frontier illnesses, possibly typhoid, dysentery, small-pox, pneumonia, or malaria.

In the summer of 1815, just a few months after his wife Polly's death, Davy married Elizabeth Patton, a relatively wealthy widow with two children described as nothing like Polly ("large, sensible, and practical.")[15] Though their marriage apparently lacked passion, Davy moved onto

---

[14] Wallis, Michael. *David Crockett: The Lion of the West*. Page 73.

Elizabeth's little farm on Bean Creek, where the couple had three children together: Robert, Rebecca and Matilda. The Crockett clan was now eight in number. Davy would spend a great part of his second marriage on hunting expeditions, as well as hunting "Indians." On one such expedition, he contracted malaria and nearly died himself.

Chapter 2: Bowie's Early Years

The Bowie Family Tree

Like so much of his life and death, even the birth of Jim Bowie (pronounced both *BOH ee* and *BOO ee*) is subject to debate. Bowie was born sometime between 1790 and 1796 in Georgia, Kentucky, or Tennessee, but due to pioneering parents who moved ever westward with the frontier, the actual date and location at the time of his birth remains uncertain, with scholars and biographers disagreeing on both details. According to the Texas State Historical Association, Jim was born in 1796 (probably on April 10) near Terrapin Creek in Kentucky to parents Rezin (or Reason) Pleasant and Elve Ap-Catesby Jones (or Johns) Bowie. In 1794, Rezin moved his family from Tennessee to Logan County, Kentucky, where he farmed and operated a gristmill with the help of eight slaves.

On the other hand, Bowie biographer Clifford Hopewell (author of *James Bowie Texas Fighting Man: A Biography*) claims that James was the ninth of ten children born to John and Elve Ap-Catesby Jones Bowie. Hopewell contends that Elve and John met when she nursed John back to health after he was seriously wounded fighting in the American Revolutionary War and married him in 1782. Moving frequently, the couple first settled in Georgia before moving to Kentucky. At the time of Jim's birth (according to Hopewell), his father owned eight slaves, eleven head of cattle, seven horses, and one stud horse. The following year, the Bowies acquired 200 acres along the Red River which they sold in 1800, after which they relocated to Missouri before moving to Spanish Louisiana in 1802, where they settled on Bushley Bayou in Rapides Parish.

Several details Hopewell provides as fact are disputed by other Bowie biographers, and no two authors seem to completely agree on the specifics of Bowie's birth and details of his early years, thus calling into question the veracity of every assertion. For example, adding to one biographical sketch, historian William C. Davis (*Three Roads to the Alamo*) numbers Jim's siblings at eight, not nine: unnamed twin girls who died in infancy in 1784, John J. (born in 1785), Sarah (1787), Mary (1789), Martha (1791), Rezin Pleasant/Rezin Jr. (1793), and Stephen (1797).

Today, it is generally accepted that the Texas State Historical Association maintains the most reliable information available, [though numerous sources dispute these claims as well].)

---

[15] Wallis, Michael. *David Crockett: The Lion of the West.* Page 134.

Regardless of when Jim was born, it is known that his family made their way to Louisiana by the beginning of the 19th century, before Thomas Jefferson purchased the land as part of the Louisiana Purchase. On May 2, 1801, Rezin Pleasant Bowie, Sr. and his brothers David, Rhesa, and John swore allegiance to the Spanish government then in control of Louisiana via land grant near present-day Rapides Parish (which would not officially be formed until 1807 by the government of the Territory of Orleans). That October, the Bowie families settled on farms in what is now Catahoula Parish, and it was there that Rezin's sons Jim, John J., Stephen, and Rezin Pleasant spent their early years.

The Bowie family is said to have taken an active part in community affairs, and Rezin reportedly became the largest slaveowner in the area with 20 slaves. Around 1809, the Bowies moved to Atakapa country and onto land settled by Native Americans calling themselves the *Ishak* (pronounced "ee-SHAK"), near the Gulf Coast of southeastern Louisiana. Rezin purchased 640 acres on the Vermilion River near the mouth of Little Bayou and established a plantation near Opelousas, where he grew cotton and sugarcane, raised livestock, and bought and sold slaves.

During Jim's teen years, he is said to have worked in Avoyelles (east-central Louisiana) and Rapides Parishes (central Louisiana), where he labored in the lumber industry, floating timber down river to market. According to the exceptionally limited biographical information currently available, Jim appears to have had no formal education whatsoever, a point no biographer seems to dispute. While history records the existence of public schools by 1808 (when the first public school was established in Pointe Coupee Parish) and institutions of higher learning by 1811 (the year the College of Orleans opened to students), there is nothing to suggest that Jim ever took advantage of the formal educational system.

Chapter 3: Bowie Becomes a Folk Hero

Speculating

During the War of 1812, Jim and his brother Rezin joined the Second Division Consolidated, a military militia unit that included the Seventeenth through Nineteenth Regiments. By this point in their lives, Jim and brother Rezin, Jr. had become inseparable and would choose the same path for most of their lives. According to a family legend passed down orally, the brothers had joined the unit in 1814 and were en route to join Andrew Jackson's forces at New Orleans, but the penultimate battle was fought before the Bowie brothers arrived. Jim would not take part in any actual military service until very near the end of his life.

Upon returning to Vermilion Bay (Vermilion Parish), Jim and his brother Rezin invested in property on the Bayou Boeuf (central Louisiana) and went into business with the infamous pirate Jean Laffite (ca. 1776--ca. 1823) and his brother Pierre, dealing in slaves. Laffite would intercept slave ships in the Gulf of Mexico and Caribbean and ran a slave market on Galveston Island, Texas, and he would bring the slaves to Bowie's Island in Vermilion Bay, after which the brothers would transport them up the Vermilion River to market in St. Landry Parish. After reaching their goal of $65,000, the brothers quit the slave-trade business.

19th century portrait purported to be Lafitte

In the mid-1820s, after leaving the slave trade, Jim and brother Rezin turned their attention to land speculation, developing friendships and business associations with many wealthy plantation owners. At the same time, they also made many enemies as well due to Jim's quick temper and growing reputation for dishonesty. According to his brother John's later recollection, "Jim had an open, frank disposition, but when aroused by an insult, his anger was terrible."

Over the next few years, brothers Steven and John joined in on the land speculation, and the Bowie Brothers speculated in land centered on the southern Louisiana parishes, where they established the Arcadia Sugar Plantation on some 1,800 acres near the town of Thibodaux. It was there that they set up the first steam-powered sugar mill in Louisiana history, and Jim is said to have bought a house in New Orleans, where he "enjoyed its excitement and pleasures", particularly gambling. Meanwhile, Rezin was elected to the Louisiana State Legislature.

In the late 1820s, Jim traveled to several eastern cities, as well as Arkansas and Mississippi (and by one account, Cuba), and upon his return he convinced his brothers that it was time to sell their holdings and find other investments. Some historians contend the decision was spurred by mounting land disputes with the U. S. Government, but other accounts suggest Jim and his brother John were drawn into a major legal inquiry over land speculation and Bowie land claims, prompted by the United States' purchase of the Louisiana Territory from France in 1803. Though delivering on its promise to honor all former land grant claims, for 20 years efforts had been made to establish who exactly owned which land in the Territory. Finally, in May 1824 Congress authorized the superior courts of each territory to hear suits from those whose claims had been "overlooked", and by late 1827 the Arkansas Superior Court received a reported 126 claims from residents claiming to have purchased land in former Spanish grants from the Bowie brothers.

Although the Superior Court originally verified most of those claims, those decisions were reversed in February of 1831 after further research revealed that the Bowie brothers had never legally acquired deeds to the lands they had bought (and sold), and that many of the deeds in question had actually been forged. In 1833, the U. S. Supreme Court upheld the reversal, but when disgruntled land investors pursued legal compensation against the Bowies, they discovered that the documents in the case had mysteriously disappeared from court records. Thus left without supportive documentation, the cases were dropped, and many former Bowie business associates naturally alleged foul play.

In 1829, Jim Bowie became engaged to 24 year old Cecelia Wells (1805-1829) in Alexandria, Louisiana, but she died on September 7, 1829, just two weeks before their wedding was to take place. On February 12, 1831, the Bowie brothers sold the Arcadia Sugar Plantation and their other landholdings, as well as a reported 82 slaves to Natchez investors, for a reported $90,000.

The "Sandbar Fight"

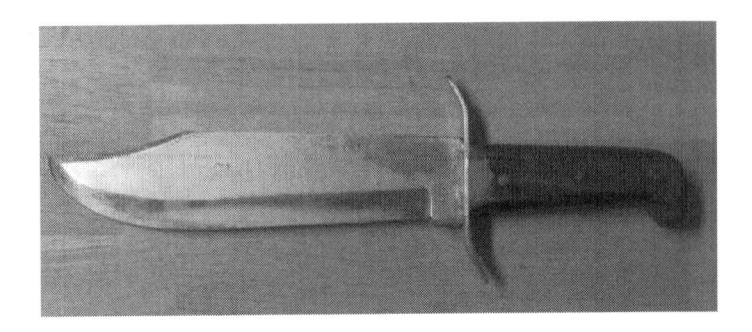

Bowie Knife

In 1827 Jim Bowie became involved in the first of many incidents that would establish him as a man of formidable audacity and fuel his growing legend.

The year before, Jim had gone to Major Norris Wright, a local banker who doubled as the sheriff of Rapides Parish, and requested a loan he desperately needed for a business venture. Wright rejected the loan, and later that year the two encountered one another in Alexandria, Louisiana. Perhaps unsurprisingly, this encounter made Jim's now-famous temper flare, and the argument between the two prompted Wright to pull a pistol and fire point-blank at Jim, only to have the bullet somehow deflect away from Bowie (perhaps by a button). According to legend, following this dangerous encounter Rezin gave Jim a large butcher-like hunting knife to carry for self-defense.

On September 19, 1827 near Natchez (Natchitoches Parish), Jim became involved in an altercation that initially started as a duel between Samuel Levi Wells III and Dr. Thomas Maddox, a shootout attended by as many as 16 men. By some accounts, Jim was serving as Wells' "second", while Rapides Parish sheriff Major Norris Wright was there to serve as Maddox's.

While it's still unclear precisely what transpired, most accounts agree that after Wells and Maddox had both fired and missed, Maddox's acquaintance Colonel Alexander Crain (some accounts list his name as Robert Crain) fired directly at Wells supporter Samuel Cuny, hitting him in the chest. An alternate account claims that Crain missed Cuny and hit Jim in the hip, knocking him to the ground. After Crain fired, Jim drew his pistol and fired at Crain but missed. Cuny and Crain then exchanged fire, with Crain hit in the arm and Cuny dying from a shot to the chest. Yet another account has Wright, not Crain, shooting Cuny in the chest.

At this point (depending upon the version of the legend), Jim is said to have drawn his knife and charged at Crain, only to be knocked to the floor by the butt of Crain's gun and then shot at (but missed) by Wright. Wright may or may not have then stabbed James with the sword of his sword-cane. Either way, Jim managed to get hold of Wright and pull him close enough to drive his knife into Wright's chest, killing the sheriff on the spot.

As Jim got to his feet, Maddox allies Carey Blanchard and Alfred Blanchard are said to have both shot at him, with one of the two hitting Jim in the arm, and some accounts describe other Maddox supporters as rushing forward to stab or shoot Jim several more times. Carey Blanchard fired a second shot at Jim but missed, and as the Blanchard brothers fled, Carey was shot and wounded by Wells supporter Major George McWhorter.

It is generally agreed that the so-called "Sandbar Fight" lasted more than ten minutes, and that Samuel Cuny and Norris Wright were left dead, and another four men were severely wounded: Alfred Blanchard, Carey Blanchard, Robert Crain, and of course, Jim Bowie. (Crain is credited with helping carry Jim to the local doctor's office.) Although there appears to be no completely reliable account of this now notorious incident, it is widely believed that while Maddox allies had ostensibly come to lend support to their colleague and business associate during his duel, they had most likely conspired to ambush Jim Bowie and those who might defend him after the duel was finished.

Though numerous versions of this encounter have been repeated for nearly two centuries, the one constant in this legend is the use of "Bowie's big butcher knife" to kill Wright. When word of his proficiency with his special blade hit the newspapers, it captured public attention, with Jim proclaimed the South's most formidable knife fighter. Though that knife now carries Bowie's name, it's widely agreed that the original "Bowie knife" was made by a man named Jesse Clifft for Jim's brother Rezin, and that it was simply designed like any other butcher knife of the day. Spanish pirates in the Gulf of Mexico also used a similar knife, and Jim's only documented use of such a knife was at the Sandbar Fight, but that was enough for a legend to be born.

A knife made for Rezin Bowie

Chapter 4: Crockett's Military Life

For the United States forces, the Creek War (also known as the Red Stick War and the Creek Civil War), began on July 27, 1813 with the Battle of Burnt Corn the southern Alabama. On August 30, 1812, a band of Creek Native Americans attacked Fort Mimms (also Mims), near modern-day Mobile, Alabama, after which a call for volunteers to defend the area was sounded. On September 20, 1813, Davy left his wife and his family to join the Second Regiment of Tennessee Volunteer Mounted Riflemen (called "Francis Jones's Company of Mounted Rifles") for an initial commitment of 90 days, serving under Colonel John Coffee. Due to his renowned abilities as a hunter, trapper, and woodsman, Private Crockett's first assignment was to conduct reconnaissance from Beatty Springs, across the Tennessee River, and into the Creek Nation.

Although Davy was assigned to reconnoiter "Red Stick" activity in the aftermath of the battle, he spent the majority of his time pillaging Native American villages, building temporary stockades, and keeping his fellow volunteers well stocked with fresh meat. Though Crockett had led many raiding parties to loot Creek stores of corn, beans, and dried beef, his fellow volunteers were comparatively inexperienced at foraging, and forced to rely on Crockett's ability to provide fresh game.)

After returning from the early engagements of the Creek War, Davy and 800 other Tennessee Volunteers went on to fight in a number of confrontations, including the Battles of Tallushatchee Village (November 3, 1813), Talledega (November 9, 1813) Fort Strother (in the Mississippi Territory in what is today St. Clair County, Alabama, in mid-November of 1813), and the Florida Expedition (1814). Davy would later write of being sickened by the scene at the Battle of Tallushatchee Village where "from the start of the assault until the last Red Stick was slaughtered, at least one hundred eighty-six Creeks were killed and about eighty more taken prisoner, mostly women and children.[16] Davy ultimately held Andrew Jackson responsible for the cruelty heaped upon the Creek people.

Davy recalled one especially gory scene during the fighting:

"We then marched to a place, which we called Camp Wills; and here it was that Captain Cannon was promoted to a colonel, and Colonel Coffee to a general. We then marched to the Ten Islands, on the Coosa river, where we established a fort; and our spy companies were sent out. They soon made prisoners of Bob Catala and his warriors, and, in a few days afterwards, we heard of some Indians in a town about eight miles off. So we mounted our horses, and put out for that town, under the direction of two friendly Creeks we had taken for pilots. We had also a Cherokee colonel, Dick Brown, and some of his men with us. When we got near the town we divided; one of our pilots going with each division. And so we passed on each side of the town, keeping near to it, until our lines met on the far side. We then closed up at both ends, so as to surround it completely; and then we sent Captain Hammond's company of rangers to bring on the affray. He had advanced near the town, when the Indians saw him, and they raised the yell, and came running at him like so many red devils. The main army was now formed in a hollow square around the town, and they pursued Hammond till they came in reach of us. We then gave them a fire, and they returned it, and then ran back into their town. We began to close on the town by making our files closer and closer, and the Indians soon saw they were our property. So most of them wanted us to take them prisoners; and their squaws and all would run and take hold of any of us they could, and give themselves up. I saw seven squaws have hold of one man, which made me think of the Scriptures. So I hollered out the Scriptures was fulfilling; that there was seven women holding to one man's coat tail. But I believe it was a hunting-shirt all the time. We took them all prisoners that came out to us in this way; but I saw some warriors run into a house, until I counted forty-six of them. We pursued them until we got near the house, when we saw a squaw sitting in the door, and she placed her feet

---

[16] Wallis, Michael. *David Crockett: The Lion of the West*. Page 112.

against the bow she had in her hand, and then took an arrow, and, raising her feet, she drew with all her might, and let fly at us, and she killed a man, whose name, I believe, was Moore. He was a lieutenant, and his death so enraged us all, that she was fired on, and had at least twenty balls blown through her. This was the first man I ever saw killed with a bow and arrow. We now shot them like dogs; and then set the house on fire, and burned it up with the forty-six warriors in it. I recollect seeing a boy who was shot down near the house. His arm and thigh was broken, and he was so near the burning house that the grease was stewing out of him. In this situation he was still trying to crawl along; but not a murmur escaped him, though he was only about twelve years old. So sullen is the Indian, when his dander is up, that he had sooner die than make a noise, or ask for quarters."

By the end of the Creek War, Andrew Jackson had defeated the Red Sticks at the Battle of Horseshoe Bend on March 27, 1814, and Davy Crockett's reputation as an Indian fighter and crack shot had become part of the frontier fabric, a legend that would follow him long after his death.

Discharged from service on March 27, 1814, Davy rejoined the Tennessee Mounted on September 28, 1814, this time entering as a non-commissioned third sergeant, to face the British at Pensacola, Florida. But rather than getting a chance to "take a crack at the 'Red Coats'", he spent most of his service scouting for lingering "Red Sticks" and foraging for food while Brig. General Andrew Jackson garnered most of the glory.

The famous portrait of Andrew Jackson (1824)

In late December 1814, Davy Crockett's time as a U. S. soldier came to an end, or so he thought. On May 21, 1815, he was elected to the position of lieutenant of the local militia, and on March 27, 1818 he was appointed Lieutenant Colonel David Crockett of the Fifty-Seventh Regiment of Tennessee Militia. It was a position he would resign in November of 1819.

Chapter 5: Crockett in Politics

Tennessee Legislature, 1821-1823

After selling a large portion of his land in Franklin County and leasing the remainder, Davy moved his family to a 160 acre tract of land in what would become Lawrence County, Tennessee made available by the "Choctaw Purchase." By the time he completed the first of three houses he would build for his family, along with a gristmill, gunpowder factory, and whiskey distillery, Davy got involved in local politics. He was soon named one of five Commissioners of the Shoal Creek Corporation, a committee charged with laying out county boundaries.

Following a series of campaign speeches enlivened with his now famous "backwoods yarns" and "homespun metaphors," on September 17, 1821 Davy Crockett was elected to the Tennessee Legislature. He was assigned to the Committee of Propositions and Grievances. This is when the larger-than-life, almost mythical dimensions of Crockett's fame began to flourish.

As legend and Davy's *Narrative* claim, during one of Davy's first days on the Tennessee Legislature floor, an event occurred involving Tennessee House member James C. Mitchell that would follow Davy throughout his political career (and add considerably to his celebrity). While arguing in opposition to a law Crockett was supporting, Mitchell sought to undermine Davy's credibility by referring to him as the "gentleman from the cane", alluding to the dense canebrakes of western Tennessee where Davy was said to hunt "b'ar" and "coons" during the winter season. But instead of having the demoralizing effect Mitchell intended, it helped instill the rough and tough, straight-talking backwoodsman image that invariably caught the imagination of his fellow citizens and would be perpetuated long past his death. From that day forward, being referred to as a "gentleman from the cane" (which actually applied to many of his fellow Tennesseans) was no longer considered derogatory but a badge of honor he and his neighbors shared.

Bear Hunter Extraordinaire

Davy may have started a political career, but he was still up for frontier life, especially when it came to hunting bears. He wrote about one especially successful bear hunting adventure in 1825:

> "In the fall of 1825, I concluded I would build two large boats, and load them with

pipe staves for market. So I went down to the lake, which was about twenty-five miles from where I lived, and hired some hands to assist me, and went to work; some at boat building, and others to getting staves. I worked on with my hands till the bears got fat, and then I turned out to hunting, to lay in a supply of meat. I soon killed and salted down as many as were necessary for my family; but about this time one of my old neighbours, who had settled down on the lake about twenty-five miles from me, came to my house and told me he wanted me to go down and kill some bears about in his parts. He said they were extremely fat, and very plenty. I know'd that when they were fat, they were easily taken, for a fat bear can't run fast or long. But I asked a bear no favours, no way, further than civility, for I now had eight large dogs, and as fierce as painters; so that a bear stood no chance at all to get away from them. So I went home with him, and then went on down towards the Mississippi, and commenced hunting.

   We were out two weeks, and in that time killed fifteen bears. Having now supplied my friend with plenty of meat, I engaged occasionally again with my hands in our boat building, and getting staves. But I at length couldn't stand it any longer without another hunt. So I concluded to take my little son, and cross over the lake, and take a hunt there. We got over, and that evening turned out and killed three bears, in little or no time. The next morning we drove up four forks, and made a sort of scaffold, on which we salted up our meat, so as to have it out of the reach of the wolves, for as soon as we would leave our camp, they would take possession. We had just eat our breakfast, when a company of hunters came to our camp, who had fourteen dogs, but all so poor, that when they would bark they would almost have to lean up against a tree and take a rest. I told them their dogs couldn't run in smell of a bear, and they had better stay at my camp, and feed them on the bones I had cut out of my meat. I left them there, and cut out; but I hadn't gone far, when my dogs took a first-rate start after a very large fat old he-bear, which run right plump towards my camp. I pursued on, but my other hunters had heard my dogs coming, and met them, and killed the bear before I got up with him. I gave him to them, and cut out again for a creek called Big Clover, which wa'n't very far off. Just as I got there, and was entering a cane brake, my dogs all broke and went ahead, and, in a little time, they raised a fuss in the cane, and seemed to be going every way. I listened a while, and found my dogs was in two companies, and that both was in a snorting fight. I sent my little son to one, and I broke for t'other. I got to mine first, and found my dogs had a two-year-old bear down, a-wooling away on him; so I just took out my big butcher, and went up and slap'd it into him, and killed him without shooting. There was five of the dogs in my company. In a short time, I heard my little son fire at his bear; when I went to him he had killed it too. He had two dogs in his team. Just at this moment we heard my other dog barking a short distance off, and all the rest immediately broke to him. We pushed on too, and when we got there, we found he had still a larger bear than either of them we had killed, treed by himself. We killed that one also, which made three we had killed in less than half an hour. We turned in and butchered them, and then started to hunt for water, and a good place to camp. But we had no sooner started, than our dogs took a start after another one, and away they went like a thunder-gust, and was out of hearing in a minute. We followed the way they had gone for some time, but at length we gave up the hope of finding them, and turned back. As we were going back, I came to where a poor fellow was grubbing, and he looked like the very picture of hard times. I asked him what he was doing away there in the woods by himself? He said he was grubbing for a man who intended to settle there; and the reason why he did it was, that he had no meat for his family, and he was working for a little.

 I was mighty sorry for the poor fellow, for it was not only a hard, but a very slow way to get meat for a hungry family; so I told him if he would go with me, I would give him more meat than he could get by grubbing in a month. I intended to supply him with meat, and also to get him to assist my little boy in packing in and salting up my bears. He had never seen a bear killed in his life. I told him I had six killed then, and my dogs were hard after another. He went off to his little cabin, which was a short distance in the brush, and his wife was very anxious he should go with me. So we started and went to where I had left my three bears, and made a camp. We then gathered my meat and salted, and scaffled it, as I had done the other. Night now came on, but no word from my dogs yet. I afterwards found they had treed the bear about five miles off, near to a man's house, and had barked at it the whole enduring night. Poor fellows! many a time they looked for me, and wondered why I didn't come, for they knowed there was no mistake in me, and I know'd they were as good as ever fluttered. In the morning, as soon as it was light enough to see, the man took his gun and went to them, and shot the bear, and killed it. My dogs, however, wouldn't have any thing to say to this stranger; so they left him, and came early in the morning back to me.

 We got our breakfast, and cut out again; and we killed four large and very fat bears that day. We hunted out the week, and in that time we killed seventeen, all of them first-rate. When we closed our hunt, I gave the man over a thousand weight of fine fat bear-meat, which pleased him mightily, and made him feel as rich as a Jew. I saw him the next fall, and he told me he had plenty of meat to do him the whole year for his week's hunt. My son and me now went home. This was the week between Christmas and New-year that we made this hunt."

Despite that successful hunt, Davy was induced to head back out for more help a neighbor who was out of meat. This time, he apparently had a more harrowing adventure:

 "In the morning I left my son at the camp, and we started on towards the harricane;

and when we had went about a mile, we started a very large bear, but we got along mighty slow on account of the cracks in the earth occasioned by the earthquakes. We, however, made out to keep in hearing of the dogs for about three miles, and then we came to the harricane. Here we had to quit our horses, as old Nick himself couldn't have got through it without sneaking it along in the form that he put on, to make a fool of our old grandmother Eve. By this time several of my dogs had got tired and come back; but we went ahead on fact for some little time in the hurricane, when we met a bear coming straight to us, and not more than twenty or thirty yards off. I started my tired dogs after him, and McDaniel pursued them, and I went on to where my other dogs were. I had seen the track of the bear they were after, and I knowed he was a screamer. I followed on to about the middle of the harricane; but my dogs pursued him so close, that they made him climb an old stump about twenty feet high. I got in shooting distance of him and fired, but I was all over in such a flutter from fatigue and running, that I couldn't hold steady; but, however, I broke his shoulder, and he fell. I run up and loaded my gun as quick as possible, and shot him again and killed him. When I went to take out my knife to butcher him, I I found I had lost it in coming through the harricane. The vines and briars was so thick that I would sometimes have to get down and crawl like a varment to get through at all; and a vine had, as I sup- posed, caught in the handle and pulled it out. While I was standing and studying what to do my friend came to me. He had followed my trail through the harricane, and had found my knife, which was mighty good news to me; as a hunter hates the worst in the world to lose a good dog, or any part of his hunting-tools. I now left McDaniel to butcher the bear, and I went after our horses, and brought them as near as the nature of case would allow. I then took our bags, and went back to where he was; and when we had skin'd the bear, we fleeced off the fat and carried it to our horses at several loads. We then packed it up on our horses, and had a heavy pack of it on each one. We now started and went on till about sunset, when I concluded we must be near our camp; so I hollered and my son answered me, and we moved on in the direction to the camp. We had gone but a little way when I heard my dogs make a warm start again; and I jumped down from my horse and gave him up to my friend, and told him I would follow them. He went on to the camp, and I went ahead after my dogs with all my might for a considerable distance, till at last night come on. The woods were very rough and hilly, and all covered over with cane.

I was compel'd to move on more slowly; and was frequently falling over logs, and into the cracks made by the earthquakes, so that I was very much afraid I would break my gun. However I went on about three miles, when I came to a good big creek, which I waded. It was very cold, and the creek was about knee-deep; but I felt no great inconvenience from it just then, as I was all over wet with sweat from running, and I felt hot enough. After I got over this creek and out of the cane, which was very thick on all our creeks, I listened for my dogs. I found they had either treed or brought the bear to a stop, as they continued barking in the same place. I pushed on as near in the direction to the noise as I could, till I found the hill was too steep for me to climb, and so I backed and went down the creek some distance till I came to a hollow, and then took up that, till I come to a place where I could climb up the hill. It was mighty dark, and was difficult to see my way or anything else. When I got up the hill, I found I had passed the dogs; and so I turned and went to them. I found, when I got there, they had treed the bear in a large forked poplar, and it was setting in the fork.

I could see the lump, but not plain enough to shoot with any cer- tainty, as there was no moonlight; and so I set in to hunting for some dry brush to make me a light; but I could find none, though I could find that the ground was torn mightily to pieces by the cracks.

At last I thought I could shoot by guess, and kill him; so I pointed as near the lump as I could, and fired away. But the bear didn't come, he only clomb up higher, and got out on a limb, which helped me to see him better. I now loaded up again and fired, but this time he didn't move at all. I commenced loading for a third fire, but the first thing I knowed, the bear was down among my dogs, and they were fighting all around me. I had my big butcher in my belt, and I had a pair of dressed buckskin breeches on. So I took out my knife, and stood, determined, if he should get hold of me, to defend myself in the best way I could. I stood there for some time, and could now and then see a white dog I had, but the rest of them, and the bear, which were dark coloured, I couldn't see at all, it was so miserable dark. They still fought around me, and sometimes within three feet of me; but, at last, the bear got down into one of the cracks, that the earthquakes had made in the ground, about four feet deep, and I could tell the biting end of him by the hollering of my dogs. So I took my gun and pushed the muzzle of it about, till I thought I had it against the main part of his body, and fired; but it happened to be only the fleshy part of his foreleg. With this, he jumped out of the crack, and he and the dogs had another hard fight around me, as before. At last, however, they forced him back into the crack again, as he was when I had shot.

I had laid down my gun in the dark, and I now began to hunt for it; and, while hunting, I got hold of a pole, and concluded I would punch him awhile with that. I did so, and when I would punch him, the dogs would jump in on him, when he would bite them badly, and they would jump out again. I concluded, as he would take punching so patiently, it might be that he would lie still enough for me to get down in the crack, and feel slowly along till I could find the right place to give him a dig with my butcher. So I got down, and my dogs got in before him and kept his head towards them, till I got along easily up to him; and placing my hand on his rump, felt for his shoulder, just behind which I intended to stick him. I made a lounge with my long knife, and fortunately stock him right through the heart; at which he just sank down, and I crawled out in a hurry. In a little time my dogs all come out too, and seemed satisfied, which was the way they always had of telling me that they had finished him.

I suffered very much that night with cold, as my leather breeches, and every thing else I had on, was wet and frozen. But I managed to get my bear out of this crack after several hard trials, and so I butchered him, and laid down to try to sleep. But my fire was very bad, and I couldn't find any thing that would burn well to make it any better; and I concluded I should freeze, if I didn't warm myself in some way by exercise. So I got up, and hollered a while, and then I would just jump up and down with all my might, and throw myself into all sorts of motions. But all this wouldn't do; for my blood was now getting cold, and the chills coming all over me. I was so tired, too, that I could hardly walk; but I thought I would do the best I could to save my life, and then, if I died, nobody would be to blame. So I went to a tree about two feet through, and not a limb on it for thirty feet, and I would climb up it to the limbs, and then lock my arms together around it, and slide down to the bottom again. This would make the insides of my legs and arms feel mighty warm and good. I continued this till daylight in the morning, and how often I clomb up my tree and slid down I don't know, but I reckon at least a hundred times.

In the morning I got my bear hong up so as to be safe, and then set out to hunt for my camp. I found it after a while, and McDaniel and my son were very much rejoiced to see me get back, for they were about to give me up for lost. We got our breakfasts, and then secured our meat by building a high scaffold, and covering it over. We had no fear of its spoiling, for the weather was so cold that it couldn't.

We now started after my other bear, which had caused me so much trouble and suffering; and before we got him, we got a start after another, and took him also. We went on to the creek I had crossed the night before and camped, and then went to where my bear was, that I had killed in the crack. When we examined the place, McDaniel said he wouldn't have gone into it, as I did, for all the bears in the woods.

We took the meat down to our camp and salted it, and also the last one we had killed; intending, in the morning, to make a hunt in the harricane again.

We prepared for resting that night, and I can assure the reader I was in need of it. We had laid down by our fire, and about ten o'clock there came a most terrible earthquake, which shook the earth so, that we were rocked about like we had been in a cradle. We were very much alarmed; for though we were accustomed to feel earthquakes, we were now right in the region which had been torn to pieces by them in 1812, and we thought it might take a notion and swallow us up, like the big fish did Jonah.

In the morning we packed up and moved to the harricane, where we made another camp, and turned out that evening and killed a very large bear, which made eight we had now killed in this hunt.

The next morning we entered the harricane again, and in little or no time my dogs were in full cry. We pursued them, and soon came to a thick cane brake, in which they had stop'd their bear. We got up close to him, as the cane was so thick that we couldn't see more than a few feet. Here I made my friend hold the cane a little open with his gun till I shot the bear, which was a mighty large one. I killed him dead in his tracks. We got him out and butchered him, and in a little time started another and killed him, which now made ten we had killed; and we know'd we couldn't pack any more home, as we had only five horses along; therefore we returned to the camp and salted up all our meat, to be ready for a start homeward next morning.

The morning came, and we packed our horses with the meat, and had as much as they could possibly carry, and sure enough cut out for home. It was about thirty miles, and we reached home the second day. I had now accommodated my neighbour with meat enough to do him, and had killed in all, up to that time, fifty-eight bears, during the fall and winter.

As soon as the time come for them to quit their houses and come out again in the spring, I took a notion to hunt a little more, and in about one month I killed forty-seven more, which made one hundred and five bears I had killed in less than one year from that time."

U. S. Congress, 1827-1833

Following his second term in the Tennessee State Legislature, Davy ran for the United States Congress. Failing to garner enough votes in 1825, he succeeded in being elected to the United States House of Representatives in 1827 and again in 1829 as a "Jacksonian" supporter of President Andrew Jackson. Interestingly, while involved in Washington politics, Davy became a Freemason, like George Washington, James Monroe, and Andrew Jackson.

After years as a Democratic Jacksonian, however, in 1828 Davy broke ties with Jackson, becoming a Whig (a party formed specifically to oppose President Andrew Jackson and his policies) for the remainder of his political career. Of the Indian Removal Bill, Crockett noted, "It was expected of me that I was to bow to the name of Andrew Jackson, and follow him in all his motions, and windings, and turnings, even at the expense of my consciences and judgment. Such a thing was new to me, and a total stranger to my principles. ... His famous, or rather I should say infamous Indian bill was brought forward and, and I opposed it from the purest motives in the world. Several of my colleagues got around me, and told me how well they loved me, and that I was ruining myself. They said it was a favorite measure of the President, and I ought to go for it. I told them I believed it was a wicked unjust measure, and that I should go against it, let the cost to myself be what it might; that I was willing to go with General Jackson in everything that I believed was honest and right; but further than this, I wouldn't go for him, or any other man in the whole creation."

As a Congressman, Davy took an unpopular position supporting the rights of "squatters" (people who occupied abandoned or unoccupied land), who were barred by law from buying land in the West without already owning property elsewhere. He also opposed President Jackson's Indian Removal Act, which would legalize the coerced removal of thousands of Cherokee, Chickasaw, Choctaw, Creek, and Seminole from the southeastern states by military force, if necessary. He also became a leading opponent of further appropriation for the United Staes Military Academy at West Point, which he saw as "an inhereantly elitist institution managed for the benefit of the nobel and wealthy of the country."[17]

When he finally had enough of the Jacksonians, he explained, "Although our great man at the head of the nation, has changed his course, I will not change mine. ... I was also a supporter of this administration after it came into power, and until the Chief Magistrate changed the principles which he professed before his election. When he quitted those principles, I quit him. I am yet a Jackson man in principles, but not in name... I shall insist upon it that I am still a Jackson man, but General Jackson is not; he has become a Van Buren man."

Crockett's open opposition to Jackson invariably led to his defeat when he ran for re-election in 1830—though he won in 1832. One often-cited quote from his political years, Davy is said to have stated resolutely, "I bark at no man's bid. I will never come and go, and fetch and carry, at the whistle of the great man in the White House no matter who he is."

Fittingly, Crockett's time as a U.S. Congressman is best remembered for a speech that he may very well not have given. Known as the "Not Yours To Give" speech, Crockett was credited with giving a speech that railed against Congress' use of taxpayers' money to help other individuals. The story, which was popularized by 19th century writer, Edward S. Ellis, has been debunked by historians. (Ellis's account is included as an appendix at the end of this book).

In 1834, Crockett's autobiography, *A Narrative of the Life of David Crockett* was published, after which he traveled east to promote the book. Though mobbed by throngs of fans wanting to get a closer look at the living legend, he was defeated for re-election, noting ruefully, "I have never knew what it was to sacrifice my own judgment to gratify any party and I have no doubt of

---

[17] Wallis, Michael. *David Crockett: The Lion of the West*. Page 217.

the time being close at hand when I will be rewarded for letting my tongue speak what my heart thinks. I have suffered myself to be politically sacrificed to save my country from ruin and disgrace and if I am never again elected I will have the gratification to know that I have done my duty."

Of this time he wrote, "I also told them of the manner in which I had been knocked down and dragged out, and that I didn't consider it a fair fight any how they could fix it. I put the ingredients in the cup pretty strong I tell you, and I concluded my speech by telling them that I was done with politics for the present, and they might all go to hell, and I would go to Texas."

Following his defeat, that's precisely what he did.

Chapter 6: Bowie in Texas

Mexican Texas

While it is unknown when Jim Bowie first entered Mexican Texas (by some accounts, 1828), it is speculated that he may have been recruited as early as 1819 in New Orleans, along with Kentucky-born Benjamin Rush "Ben" Milam (1788-1835), who would become a leading figure of the Texas Revolution.

Ben Milam

On January 1, 1830, Jim and Isaac Donoho left Thibodaux for Texas, stopping in San Felipe to present a letter of introduction to empresario Stephen F. Austin from Thomas F. McKinney, one of the Old Three Hundred colonists. The "Old Three Hundred" were the 297 grantees - families and partnerships of unmarried men - who purchased 307 parcels of land from Austin and established a colony encompassing an area of land from the Gulf of Mexico to near present-day Brenham in Washington County in Texas, Navasota in Grimes County, and La Grange in Fayette County. Moses Austin was the original empresario of the Old Three Hundred and was succeeded by his son Stephen after his untimely death.

Stephen Austin

On February 20, Jim (now 34 years old by most accounts) and Isaac Donoho took the Oath of Allegiance to Mexico and set off for San Antonio, along with Mr. and Mrs. William H. Wharton, Caiaphas K. Ham, and several slaves, delivering letters of introduction to two wealthy and influential Mexicans, Juan Martín de Veramendi and Juan N. Seguín. After that they continued on to Saltillo, the state capital of *Coahuila y Tejas* (Coahuila and Texas), one of the constituent states of the newly established United Mexican States under its 1824 Constitution.

In Saltillo, Jim learned that a Mexican law enacted in 1828 offered its citizens 11 league grants in Texas for $100-$250 each (a league equals 4,428.4 acres). Bowie urged Mexicans to apply for the 11 league grants, which he then purchased from them. Leaving Saltillo with 15 or 16 of these grants, he continued to encourage speculation in Texas lands, activities that irritated Stephen F. Austin so much that he at first hesitated to approve lands Bowie wanted to include in the Austin colony. Ultimately Austin relented and approved.

While residing in San Antonio, Bowie is said to have posed as a man of wealth, ingratiating himself with the wealthy de Veramendi family and even convincing them to sponsor his baptism into the Catholic Church. The 1824 Constitution of Mexico banned religions other than Roman Catholicism and gave preference to Mexican citizens in land grants, so it's apparent why Bowie would take such a step.

In the fall of 1830 Jim accompanied the de Veramendi family to Saltillo, officially becoming a Mexican citizen on October 5, with his citizenship contingent on his establishing wool and cotton mills in Coahuila. With the help of friend and associate Angus McNeill of Natchez, Jim purchased a textile mill for $20,000.

The following year, Jim married Ursula de Veramendi in San Antonio, and when he appeared before the mayor, he declared his age to be 32 (though he was probably 35), and pledging to pay Ursula a dowry of $15,000. Though he valued his personal wealth and properties at $222,800, the titles to his 60,000 arpents (a French unit of measurement used in Louisiana, Mississippi, Alabama, and Florida, 1 arpent = 0.84628-acre) of Arkansas land, valued at $30,000, were proven fraudulent. And though he was owed $45,000 for his interest in the Arcadia Sugar Plantation, Jim ultimately had to borrow nearly $2000 from his father-in-law and $750 from his wife's grandmother to afford a honeymoon in New Orleans and Natchez.

Upon their return, James and Ursela Bowie built a house in San Antonio on land de Veramendi had given them near the San José Mission, but after a short time they moved into the de Veramendi Palace and lived with Ursula's parents, who reportedly supplied them with money as needed.

There are many conflicting accounts of the Bowie family in Mexican Texas, but it's believed the couple had two children: Marie Elve (b. March 20, 1832) and James Veramendi (b. July 18, 1833). Neither apparently survived to adulthood.

The "Lost" Los Almagres Mine

According to de Veramendi family oral tradition, Jim spent little time at home once married, apparently fascinated by the legend of the "lost" Los Almagres Mine said to be located west of San Antonio near the ruin of Santa Cruz de San Sabá Mission. Discovered in 1753 by a small group of Spaniards who excavated a test pit at this site, it was initially occupied by Apache. Obtaining permission from Mexican authorities for an expedition into "Indian Country," Jim convinced his father-in-law to bankroll the endeavor, leaving San Antonio with his brother Rezin and nine others on November 2, 1831.

On November 19, Bowie learned that a large Apache war party was following the expedition, so he opted to set up camp six miles from San Saba and attempt a parley, which quickly escalated into an exchange of gunfire. After a reported 13 hours, the Apache finally withdrew, said to have left 40 dead and 30 wounded behind, while Bowie's party had lost one man and several wounded. Failing to reach their destination, the party returned to San Antonio.

On January 23, 1832, Bowie made another foray to the west, this time carrying the title of "colonel" of citizen rangers. Leaving Gonzales with 26 men to scout the headwaters of the Colorado for Tawakonis and other "hostile Indians," after a fruitless two and a half-month search he returned home.

The Battle of Nacogdoches

The Battle of Nacogdoches, sometimes called the "opening gun" of the Texas Revolution, occurred on August 2, 1832, when a group of Texas settlers defied an order by Colonel José de las Piedras, commander of the Mexican Twelfth Permanent Battalion at Nacogdoches, to surrender their arms.

In July 1832, while visiting Natchez, Colonel Bowie learned that José de las Piedras had visited the towns of Anahuac and Velasco in an effort to quiet mounting tension between the Mexican government and Anglo Texas settlers. Upon his return, Piedras demanded that all citizens in his jurisdiction surrender their arms, a demand the colonists rejected. Bowie hurried to Nacogdoches, and on August 1 he accompanied James W. Bullock and 300 armed men during their siege of the garrison there, resulting in what became known as the Battle of Nacogdoches (August 2, 1832). Though Piedras initially chose to fight, by nightfall he was forced to evacuate his men, leaving 33 dead behind, after Bowie and 18 of his men ambushed the Mexican column and put Piedras to flight.

On March 9, 1833, Monclova replaced Saltillo as the state capital, resulting in the two towns raising small armies to contest the change. Bowie favored Monclova, though some accounts claim he was a mercenary. On one occasion when the forces confronted each other, Bowie is said to have rode out and tried to instigate a fight, believing that the fortunes of Texas land speculators lay with Monclova, but there is still controversy surrounding the accuracy of this account.

Death Strikes

In August 1833, after a cholera epidemic struck Texas, Jim sent his wife and possibly his daughter to Monclova to escape the disease, but the epidemic unexpectedly struck Monclova the following month, killing de Veramendi and his wife Josefa as well as Ursula Bowie (and perhaps their daughter). De Veramendi oral tradition states that Ursula and one Bowie child died in the epidemic, while Bowie family tradition asserts that two Bowie children died. Either way, Jim did not see his family before their deaths because he was also ill with yellow fever in Natchez, and he remained unaware of their deaths until his recovery.

On October 31, Jim dictated his last will and testament, bequeathing half of his estate to his brother Rezin, and half to his sister Martha Sterrett and her husband. It's believed that this second "half" may have actually been worth nothing whatsoever.

Commissioner of Settlement

With the coffers of the Mexican Treasury nearly empty by 1834, that year and the next laws were passed to promote wholesale speculation in Texas lands. Bowie was subsequently appointed a commissioner to promote settlement in land purchased by John T. Mason, who represented the Galveston Bay and Texas Land Company interests. Before the deal was sealed, however, colonists became incensed about large 400 league parcels being handed out by the governor for frontier defense and rumors that San Antonio was to be made the capital, and Bowie's handling of Mason's 400-league purchase was called into question. Colonists began to distrust the legitimacy of the land they'd purchased.

In May 1834, in an effort towards establishing his dictatorship, President Antonio de Padua María Severino López de Santa Anna ordered disarmament of the civic militia and suggested to Mexican Congress that they should abolish the controversial Ley del Caso (Case Law) passed in June of 1833 that effectively ordered opponents of the reformist regime (established under President Santa Anna and Vice President Valentín Gómez Farías) into exile. The following year, after Santa Anna defeated the "Zacatecan militia" (the largest and best supplied opposition of the Mexican states, led by Francisco García) and took almost 3,000 prisoners, Santa Anna abolished the *Coahuila y Tejas* government and ordered the arrest of all Texans doing business in Monclova. With the subsequent adoption of the 1835 "Constitutional Bases", through which the federal republic was converted into a singular entity, Santa Anna attempted to centralize the government by splitting the State of *Coahuila y Teja* in two: the Department of Coahuila and the Department of Texas. When news reached Jim Bowie, he fled the capital for Texas to avoid arrest.

Portrait of Santa Anna

Preparation for War

By June 1835, all communication between Mexico and Texas had been cut off, Texas Army troops were boarding ships at Matamoros for the Texas coast, and Mexican forces were en route from Saltillo to the Rio Grande. In July, with both Coahuila and Texas planning to secede from Mexico rather than fall under Santa Anna's centralized government, Jim Bowie and others in San Felipe and Nacogdoches prepared for war. Bowie's first overt act of war was to lead a small group of Texas militia to San Antonio and seize a stockpile of muskets from the Mexican armory.

On July 31, 1835, American lawyer and leader of the Texas "War Party" William Barret Travis wrote to Jim to inform him that Texians were divided and that the "Peace Party" formed in 1832 to seek peaceful means to resolve conflict appeared the stronger of the two. Travis, who had abandoned his wife, son, and unborn daughter when he departed for Texas, was already a Texas

Army lieutenant colonel.

Painting of Travis by H.A. McArdle

The events of 1835, which displayed the increasingly centralized nature of Antonio López de Santa Anna's regime, began to more clearly delineate the lines between the so-called "War" and "Peace" factions, but with the Peace faction still going strong, Bowie started trying to persuade them to become more bellicose. In an effort to garner support for Travis and the "War Party," Bowie visited several Native American villages in East Texas in an attempt to persuade the reluctant tribes to fight against the Mexican government, while Santa Anna responded to the insurrection by ordering large numbers of Mexican troops to Texas.

Chapter 7: The Start of the Texas Revolution

Battle of Concepción

On September 1, 1835, "Father of Texas" Steven F. Austin, who had led the earliest successful colonization of the Texas region with his father Moses, returned after a long imprisonment in Mexico City, and the following month the Texas Revolution was ignited with the Battle of Gonzales. In early October of 1835, a group of Texian volunteers repelled a force of Mexican cavalry led by Lieutenant Francisco de Castañeda, which had been tasked with reclaiming a cannon given to the people of Gonzales in 1831. This officially opened the Texas Revolution. The residents of Gonzales kept their cannon, and the victory swelled the Texians' ranks to 300 men. Stephen F. Austin was selected to command the small army. Upon being elected to command the volunteer army in resistance to Santa Anna's Mexican forces, Austin issued a call to arms, camping his men on Cibolo Creek 20 miles from San Antonio on October 16. Upon arrival, Jim Bowie was recruited to Austin's staff as a colonel in the volunteer militia.

On October 22, Austin asked Colonel Bowie and Colonel James W. Fannin, Jr. to scout the area around the missions of San Francisco de la Espada and San José y San Miguel de Aguayo for supplies for the volunteer forces. Discovering a prime defensive position at San Francisco de la Espada Mission near Mission Concepción, and driving off a Mexican patrol in the process, Bowie and Fannin recommended that Commander Austin bring his army of 400 men there. On October 26, Austin did as suggested.

On the morning of October 28, as fog covered the ground, Mexican General Domingo Ugartechea led a force of about 300 infantry and cavalry soldiers and two small cannon against Austin's Texian insurgent forces. Although the Mexican army was able to get within 200 yards of the fortification, the Texian defensive position protected them well from fire. At one point when the Mexicans stopped to reload their cannon, the Texians seized the opportunity to climb a bluff and pick off some of the soldiers with sharpshooters. After three hours, the standoff finally ended when Colonel Bowie led a charge to seize one of the Mexican cannon, forcing Ugartechea to withdraw his troops. When the smoke finally cleared, one Texian and 10 Mexican troops were dead. Bowie then captured a six-pounder cannon and 30 muskets. Bowie, Fannin, and a detachment remained in the immediate area south of San Antonio de Béxar while Austin moved his army and established headquarters on the Alamo Canal.

Noah Smithwick, one of the men under Bowie's command later praised Bowie as a "born leader," writing that he was "never needlessly spending a bullet or imperiling a life. His voice is still ringing in my old deaf ears as he repeatedly admonished us. 'Keep under cover boys and reserve your fire; we haven't a man to spare.'"[18]

"Not an Officer of the Government Nor Army"

Three days after the Battle of Concepción, Commander Austin sent Travis and 50 men to capture some 900 Mexican horses being driven south to Laredo and asked Colonel Bowie to create a diversion to cover the escape of Mexican soldiers who might want to desert. But though Bowie made a display of force as ordered, no Mexican soldiers joined them as expected.

On October 31, 1835, Bowie notified Mexican General Martín Perfecto de Cos that he was planning to join Commander Austin in an attack on Bexar, with Austin demanding de Cos surrender on November 1. De Cos refused, and the following day Austin's officers voted 44 to 3 against storming San Antonio de Béxar, with Bowie declining to vote. Instead, Bowie asked to

---

[18] Edmondson, J. R. *The Alamo Story-From History to Current Conflicts*. Page 223.

be relieved of command, citing that while he had previously served in a volunteer ranger group and was prepared to serve the community in time of need, he had little interest in a formal command. Though Provisional Governor Henry Smith and Sam Houston wanted him to raise a volunteer militia to attack Matamoros, the General Council declared that Bowie was not "an officer of the government nor army."[19]

The Grass Fight

The army grew to over 600 troops with the arrival of volunteers from East Texas led by Thomas J. Rusk, but as the weather turned cold, some Texian troops left camp for winter clothing. Those who left were quickly replaced by more East Texas reinforcements. Occasional cavalry skirmishes occurred as the Texians scouted for Mexican supply trains and maintained a long-range picket against General Cos's troops. William Barret Travis and a small cavalry force captured some 300 Mexican mules and horses grazing in pastures west of the Medina River about 30 miles west of the Alamo, and shortly afterwards Colonel Ugartechea departed from San Antonio de Béxar with a cavalry escort to guide Mexican reinforcements north from the Rio Grande River. The unusually cold weather of Fall and Winter of 1835-36 exacerbated supply shortages and caused morale problems among all troops, Mexican and Texian.

In mid-November, over 100 volunteers from the United States arrived in the Texian camp. Austin planned an attack and attempted to rally his troops for an attack on San Antonio de Béxar, but again his officers balked. Following this episode, Austin left for diplomatic duty in the United States, and Edward Burleson assumed command of the Texian army. Meanwhile, Bowie left for a brief trip to San Felipe, and when he returned to San Antonio on November 18, he learned that a shipment of silver coming from Mexico was being transported on a train of pack mules on its way to pay the soldiers of Mexican General Cos. Texas scouts kept a close watch for the convoy so that the gold might be intercepted, which would not only help fund their military but serve to undermine Cos' troops' morale, and on the morning of November 28 Texian "Deaf" Erastus Smith discovered a train loaded with pack mules approaching while on patrol. Suspecting this was the awaited train, he reported his discovery to Bowie, who led a group of 30 horsemen and intercepted the train and its cavalry escort.

In the resulting skirmish, known as the "Grass Fight", Bowie fought off several assaults by Mexican infantry until 100 reinforcements under Colonel Ed Burleson arrived, after which the Texians routed the Mexican defenders and forced them to abandon their mules and cargo. However, when the Texians examined the mule packs, they discovered they were filled with grass, apparently for the garrison's livestock.

Bowie subsequently proceeded to Goliad, Texas to assess the conditions there, and during his absence Colonel Burleson attacked San Antonio de Béxar on December 5. By early December,

---

[19] Texas State Historical Association, *The Handbook of Texas Online*, "Bowie, James."

Burleson had been considering withdrawing and moving the army to a winter bivouac near Goliad, but the surrender of a Mexican officer who reported that there was low morale among the Mexican troops led Burleson to plan an attack on the town. While James C. Neill directed artillery fire on the Mexican positions, Benjamin Milam and Francis Johnson led two columns that seized houses north of the Alamo plaza in the pre-dawn hours of December 5. In four days of house-to-house fighting, the Texians managed to destroy buildings near the plaza and capture several more houses, including the priest's house on the main plaza. On December 8, Colonel Ugartechea returned with over 600 reinforcements, but of these, less than 200 were experienced soldiers and all were poorly equipped. Later that day, as General Cos attempted to consolidate his forces, four companies of cavalry deserted, disobeying their orders and abandoning the beleaguered Mexican troops. The following morning, Cos approached the Texian commander asking for surrender terms. Burleson received the surrender of the Mexican equipment and weapons but allowed Cos to lead his troops back to Mexico; neither army could support a large group of prisoners. As Cos and his men departed San Antonio de Béxar and traveled south, the Texian army began to break-up, and most of the men left for their homes. The Texian army had gained control of San Antonio de Béxar, the Alamo, and the rest of Texas.

While the bulk of the volunteer troops who had taken San Antonio de Béxar rested at home, James C. Neill was given command of the Texian troops remaining in the town due to his experience as an artillery officer and his commission in the regular army (he had been commissioned as a Lieutenant Colonel in early December). Neill set about strengthening the Alamo's defensive fortifications and had most of the settlement's 21 artillery pieces emplaced on the fort's walls. Though Major Green Jameson (one of Neill's officers) would boast that the fort's artillery could repel attackers at a rate of ten to one, the Alamo's commander was less optimistic. Lieutenant Colonel Neill wrote to General Sam Houston in mid-January detailing the manpower and supply shortages at San Antonio de Béxar, describing his troops as defenseless, and warning that the fort would easily be overwhelmed by a determined attack. San Antonio de Béxar was far from the majority of the other Texas settlements and lacking local sources of food, fodder, and arms to support the garrison the troops there suffered from resupply difficulties.

Sam Houston

Soon after receiving Neill's letter, Houston began to wonder whether the San Antonio de Béxar garrison was sustainable, and he wrote to Governor Henry Smith requesting permission to abandon the Alamo, destroy its fortifications, and withdraw its troops and artillery to Gonzales and Copano. After receiving Neill's letter, Houston dispatched James Bowie with orders to assess the situation and assist in the destruction of the fort and the withdrawal of men and equipment. Upon his arrival, Bowie was impressed by Neill's preparations and wrote to Smith exhorting the Alamo's commander and praising his work. Moreover, the defenders thought that a lack of ability to evacuate the artillery made destroying the Alamo and retreating futile. On January 26, the Alamo's defenders debated and signed a resolution in favor of staying to defend the Alamo.

Among Neill's chief complaints was his inability to send out mounted scouts for lack of horses. Though Smith professed to want to reinforce the Alamo, his response was half-hearted, and he called for a "Legion of Cavalry" to accompany Lieutenant Colonel William B. Travis to San Antonio de Béxar. 30 men responded, and after protesting that he was risking his reputation, Travis agreed to lead the cavalry troops to San Antonio de Béxar. In early February, Travis and his small cavalry escort arrived at the Alamo, and like Bowie, Travis was soon converted and pledged his allegiance to Neill and the Alamo, which the defenders began to regard as the "key to Texas."

Crockett Heads to Texas

"I leave this rule for others when I'm dead
Be always sure you're right — THEN GO AHEAD!" -

By December of 1834, Davy had become so dissatisfied with the direction U. S. politics was heading that he wrote friends saying that if Martin Van Buren (Jackson's Vice President) were elected President, he was prepared to move to Texas. The next year, he helped raise a company of volunteers to take to Texas, assuming that a revolution was imminent.

After it was announced that Van Buren had gotten the nomination, in November of 1835, Davy traveled to Jackson, Tennessee with 30 well-armed men, where he addressed a crowd of local residents from the steps of the Madison County courthouse and then rode southwest to Memphis. After arriving there in the second week of November, he continued his journey to Arkansas. When Davy arrived in Little Rock, Arkansas on November 12, 1835, he was met by hundreds of people wanting to get a look at famous Crockett. A group of the town's leading citizens put on a dinner in his honor at the Jeffries Hotel where Crockett spoke about Washington politics and the prospect of Texan independence.

In early January of 1836, Davy and his volunteers arrived in Nacogdoches, Texas, where on January 14, 1836 he and 65 other mercenaries signed an oath before the Provisional Government of Texas, swearing to serve a six-month stint in the Voluntary Auxiliary Corps of the Texas Army. Crockett, promised 4000 acres of land and eligibility to hold State office, stated, "I have taken the oath of government and have enrolled my name as a volunteer and will set out for the Rio Grande in a few days with the volunteers from the United States."[20]

Just before reaching Nacogdoches, Davy had begun drafting a letter to his daughter Margaret in Tennessee. Penned just two months before his death, it is believed to be Davy's last correspondence.)

---

[20] Wallis, Michael. *David Crockett: The Lion of the West*. Page 290.

In early February 1836, Crockett and a few men headed to San Antonio de Bexar and made camp, where they were met by Bowie and Antonio Menchaca and taken to the home of Don Erasmo Seguin. Crockett and the small company of American volunteers he was with arrived at the Alamo on February 8. The defenders of Alamo now numbered some 200 men.

In mid-February, Neill received word that his family had been struck by an illness, and he was needed in Bastrop. When the commander departed he left Travis in command of the garrison, ensuring the troops he would return within three weeks. Without intending to do so, Neill had insulted the proud Bowie and angered the Texas volunteer troops who were used to "electing" their officers. On the other hand, Neill's decision made military sense; despite being younger than Bowie, Travis held a commission as regular army officer, while Bowie, on the other hand, held only the "volunteer" rank of Colonel.

Rankled and vocal, the Texas volunteers began to agitate for an "election," to allow them to choose their commander. Travis acquiesced, and the garrison voted largely along party lines. The regular army troops voted for Travis, while the volunteers voted for Bowie. In response, Bowie went on a drunken tear through the town, confiscating private property and freeing prisoners from the jail. Shocked by Bowie's alcohol-fueled display, Travis moved his men to the Medina River area about 15 miles away and wrote to Governor Smith, describing the situation as "awkward." Soon after Bowie's "celebration," news reached the Alamo that General Antonio López de Santa Anna, the autocratic president of Mexico and the commander of the nation's military forces, was approaching the Rio Grande River with a large army. Faced with the gravity of their situation, the two men put aside personality differences and came to a compromise.

Bowie would command the volunteers, Travis would command the regular army troops, and the co-commanders would consult on decisions and report to Neill together.

Chapter 8: The Alamo

The History of the Alamo

"You can plainly see that the Alamo never was built by a military people for a fortress." Letter from engineer Green B. Jameson to Sam Houston, dated January 18, 1836.

Drawing of the chapel in the 1850s depicting how it would've looked in 1836

The historical site commonly known as "The Alamo" was originally founded as a Spanish mission, named San Antonio de Valero, by Father Antonio de San Buenaventura y Olivares, nine years after he first visited the area in 1709. Olivares sought permission to found a mission in the central Texas region and was granted a mandate in 1716 to move a failing mission located on the Rio Grande River near present day Guerrero, Coahuila, Mexico (roughly twenty-five miles southeast of Eagle Pass, Texas). The plan was for that mission to be moved to Béxar, the present day San Antonio area, as part of five missions founded along the San Antonio River.

On May 1, 1718, the original mission was founded northwest of the present location, near San Pedro Springs. By 1724, when the majority of the mission's buildings were damaged by a hurricane, the Franciscans began construction at the present site near the San Antonio River. The original buildings were temporary and none have survived, but in 1727 work began on a stone building that was intended to become the *convento*, or priests' residence. The completed plan would have featured a cruciform layout, a barrel-vaulted roof, a cupola or dome over the crossing, and twin bell towers flanking the ornate façade. However, the third story of the structure was never even started, and neither were the bell towers. Four stone arches were built to support the dome, but the dome itself was never constructed. Though it never wound up being used for religious services, the chapel itself was decorated with statues on each side of the door, including statues of St. Francis, St. Dominic, St. Clare and St. Margaret of Cortona.

Before the mission could be completed, the mission was beset by repeated setbacks throughout the 1730s and 1740s, including attacks by Apaches and their allies and a smallpox epidemic that struck the area in 1739. During its time as a working mission, San Antonio de Valero served and ministered to Native Americans from over 100 bands, including Apaches and Karankawas. The middle decades of the eighteenth century saw the mission's most success in evangelizing and recruiting indigenous people, and the Native American population of the mission peaked in 1756. But as the mission's Native American population declined, progress on the mission's construction slowed to a crawl.

In 1773, the Franciscans of Querétaro (the overseers of San Antonio de Valero) transferred administration of the area's missions to the Franciscans of the College of Nuestra Señora de Guadalupe de Zacatecas. 20 years later, the Spanish colonial government ordered San Antonio de Valero secularized at the request of the Franciscans of the College of Nuestra Señora de Guadalupe de Zacatecas. Religious offices and responsibilities passed to the nearby parish of San Fernando de Béxar, and the mission's possessions (lands, houses, tools, seeds, and livestock) were distributed among the remaining Native Americans and other settlers.

The Texas missions often had to provide for their defense because the Spanish colonial government posted insufficient troops at the San Antonio de Béxar Presidio. After the 1758 massacre at Mission Santa Cruz de San Sabá (about 140 miles north of the Alamo), defensive walls and a fortified gate were added. The eight foot high and two foot thick walls were constructed around the plaza just west of the convento, adding to the mission's military value, and during the early 19th century the old mission would serve as quarters for military units and as the settlement's first hospital.

In early 1803, La Segunda Compañia Volante de San Carlos de Parras (Álamo de Parras) arrived in Texas and were quartered in the San Antonio de Valero mission building with orders to suppress Native American raiding and deal with other criminal activity. Fears of a possible invasion by U.S. military forces in the wake of Spain's return of the Louisiana Territory to France also led to the posting of the company of 100 lancers to Béxar area. La Compañia del Álamo (the unit's unusually long formal name was shortened in common use) established Béxar's first hospital in the former mission in 1805. Through its association with the cavalry unit the mission began to be referred to as El Álamo, which was another common name for the Spanish company of lancers. In addition to giving the Alamo its name, La Compañia del Álamo also added to Béxar's population as the soldiers and their families settled in the mission-turned-fort. Over the ensuing years, men from the unit married members of the surrounding Béxar community and soon the area immediately around the Alamo began to be referred as *el barrio del Álamo*.

La Compañia del Álamo increased the size of the fort's enclosure in 1809 in response to perceived invasion threats, and members of the company participated in action during the Casas Revolt of 1811, assisting in the capture of Governor Juan Bautista de las Casas. Later, José Bernardo Gutiérrez de Lara sought assistance from the United States for the anti-royalist Mexican cause and crossed the Sabine River into Texas in early August of 1812 accompanied by Lieutenant Augustus W. Magee and a company of about 125 men. As the company moved through Texas defeating small royalist detachments, the column recruited both American and Mexican volunteers. The mixed force of Mexican revolutionary insurgents and Americans commanded by Samuel Kemper (Magee was killed earlier in the campaign) occupied Béxar with nearly a thousand troops in early April, 1813. Governor Manuel María de Salcedo, commanding the royalist troops at both the San Antonio de Béxar Presidio and the Alamo, surrendered his command unconditionally to the leaders of the Gutierrez/Magee Expedition. Some of the lancers, including their commander, joined the invading force.

After the capture of San Antonio de Béxar, Gutierrez de Lara allowed the execution of General Salcedo and over a dozen other royalist officers. His action disturbed many of the American volunteers, and led by Kemper, a group of roughly 100 promptly departed San Antonio de Béxar for Louisiana on "furlough." San Antonio de Béxar was soon recaptured by the royalist forces, who executed over 300 residents in reprisal. A similar bloodbath occurred in Nacogdoches.

In the aftermath of the Gutierrez/Magee expedition, the military presence at the Alamo slowly degenerated into an ineffectual constabulary force, leaving the settlement open to unimpeded raids by Native Americans and various bandits. The old fort was largely abandoned, and the continuing Mexican War of Independence delayed efforts to re-occupy the Alamo and rebuild the Spanish military in general.

In late 1817, colonial Governor Antonio Martinez issued orders to reconstitute the Álamo de Parras Company of lancers in an effort to rebuild Spain's military presence in Texas, and he detached 75 veterans from the company of Nuestra Señora del Carmen to occupy the Alamo. Upon arriving in San Antonio de Béxar, the company's ranks were filled out with local conscripts. After the close of the Mexican War of Independence, the Álamo de Parras Company, now a Mexican military unit, remained posted at the Alamo in San Antonio de Béxar.

In 1830, the company was moved to Fort Tenoxtitlan as part of an effort to counter illegal immigration into Mexican Texas, control smuggling, and increase colonization. General Manuel de Mier y Terán planned the establishment of a series of outposts on the Texas frontier and envisioned Fort Tenoxtitlan as the future capital of the Mexican state of Texas. The Nahuatl word *Tenoxtitlan* for the Aztec city-state, now Mexico City, means *the place of the prickly pears*. The men of the Álamo de Parras Company built Fort Tenoxtitlan on the Brazos River just off of the Old San Antonio road, east of present-day Caldwell, Texas and roughly 150 miles northeast of San Antonio de Béxar.

However, civil war in Mexico City and the lack of support for Mier y Terán's colonization plan for Texas resulted in the deterioration of the system of outposts. In late July, General Mier y Terán, disconsolate due to the failure of his colonization plan, committed suicide, and the fort was finally abandoned in August of 1832. The soldiers and their families arrived in San Antonio de Béxar in mid-September and most immediately joined a column of troops moving south to Matamoros. Of the few company members who remained in San Antonio de Béxar, some left the company, pushed by the government's neglect of the Alamo garrison and the political climate, further depleting the unit's ranks. Soldiers left both by formal resignation and desertion, and some joined the burgeoning Texas revolutionary army. The tiny remnant of the Álamo de Parras Company occupying the Alamo assisted General Martín Perfecto de Cos and his forces in the defense of San Antonio de Béxar during the Siege of Béxar, and Cos surrendered the Alamo to the Texas revolutionary forces on December 11, 1835. Cos and his forces were allowed to retreat to Monclova, ending the occupation of the San Antonio de Valero mission by the Álamo de Parras company and leaving the mission its iconic name.

The Siege

Santa Anna crossed the Rio Grande River on February 16, 1836, and soon it became apparent that his target was San Antonio de Béxar. Santa Anna was likely motivated by a desire to exact revenge on the Texian rebels who had forced his brother-in-law, General Cos, to surrender the Alamo in December 1835, but record low temperatures and an unheard of fifteen inches of snow in south Texas hampered the Mexican column's advance north toward the Béxar area.

By February 21, Santa Anna and the lead elements of his column had reached the Medina River, about 30 miles west of the Alamo, and the General canceled a surprise cavalry attack planned for February 22 due to heavy rains. Probably based on the severe weather, Travis estimated that Santa Anna and his column would not arrive in San Antonio de Béxar until mid-March, so Travis and Bowie were understandably surprised when the vanguard of Santa Anna's column arrived in the Béxar area on February 23, 1836. Travis dashed off a quick message to the Texians at Gonzales, some 70 miles away, asking for resupply and reinforcement and describing the disposition of the enemy as numerous and nearby. Travis sent off a courier with a letter stating, "The enemy in large force is in sight... We want men and provisions ... Send them to us. We have 150 men & are determined to defend the Alamo to the last." When the Mexicans raised a flag indicating that they would give no quarter, Travis had a cannon shot fired at it.

However, unbeknownst to Travis, Bowie had taken it upon himself to unilaterally parley with the Mexicans. Bowie met with Colonel Juan Almonte to negotiate surrender terms, to which the

Mexicans replied, "I reply to you, according to the order of His Excellency, that the Mexican army cannot come to terms under any conditions with rebellious foreigners to whom there is no recourse left, if they wish to save their lives, than to place themselves immediately at the disposal of the Supreme Government from whom alone they may expect clemency after some considerations." Without consulting Travis, Bowie flatly refused the unconditional terms despite the Mexican threat of no quarter should the Texians refuse the surrender terms, though after he returned to the Alamo, he and Travis both agreed not to surrender. Once again, the defenders answered with another volley from the fort's 18 pound cannon.

On February 24, 1836, Bowie fell ill from a sickness that was described as "hasty consumption" and "typhoid pneumonia". He was likely suffering from advanced tuberculosis. Regardless, Bowie retreated to his quarters and ended up remaining there during the rest of the siege, including the culminating battle. With that, the leadership issues had been resolved, and Travis assumed full command of the small force occupying the Alamo. That same day, Travis penned an open letter to the Texans and Americans that was both intended to be a rallying cry and a request for reinforcements:

> To the People of Texas & All Americans in the World:
>
> Fellow citizens & compatriots—I am besieged, by a thousand or more of the Mexicans under Santa Anna—I have sustained a continual Bombardment & cannonade for 24 hours & have not lost a man. The enemy has demanded a surrender at discretion, otherwise, the garrison are to be put to the sword, if the fort is taken—I have answered the demand with a cannon shot, & our flag still waves proudly from the walls. I shall never surrender or retreat. Then, I call on you in the name of Liberty, of patriotism & everything dear to the American character, to come to our aid, with all dispatch—The enemy is receiving reinforcements daily & will no doubt increase to three or four thousand in four or five days. If this call is neglected, I am determined to sustain myself as long as possible & die like a soldier who never forgets what is due to his own honor & that of his country—Victory or Death.
>
> William Barret Travis
>
> Lt. Col. comdt
>
> P.S. The Lord is on our side—When the enemy appeared in sight we had not three bushels of corn—We have since found in deserted houses 80 or 90 bushels & got into the walls 20 or 30 head of Beeves.
>
> Travis

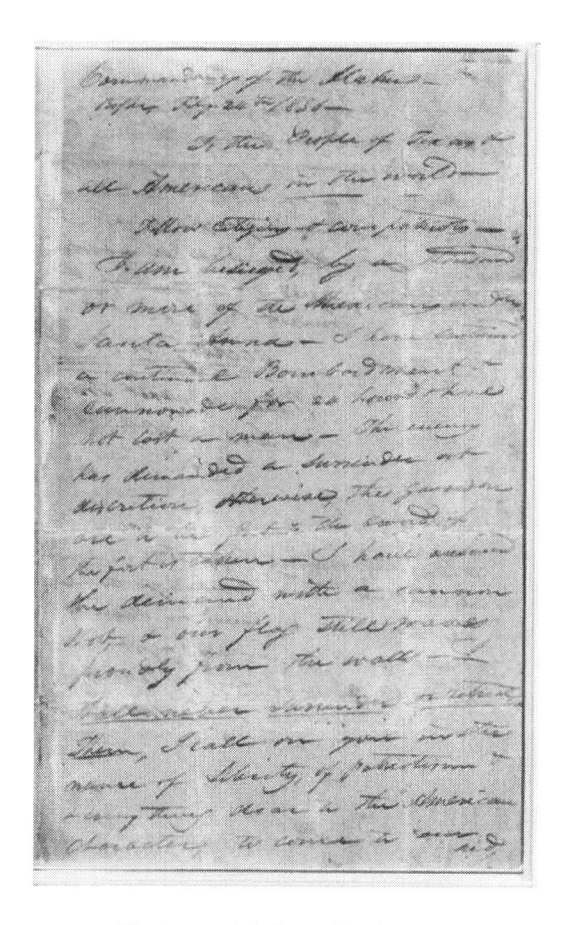

First page of the letter Travis wrote

    The young commander estimated his enemy would number three to four thousand troops in four or five days, and one can assume he learned that the Alamo's defenders would be "put to the sword" from Bowie, who had earlier refused the surrender terms the Mexicans offered the Texians. Even if Bowie's parley hadn't made that clear, the men behind the Alamo's ramparts probably heard Santa Anna's forces playing the fifth and final part of a sequence of bugle orders for cavalry called "El De Guello" and flying the red flag of no quarter. The short song was the culmination of the bugle call ordering Mexican cavalry to commence an attack, and the pace of the music dictated the pace of the charging cavalry troopers. The mournful tune "De Guello," was planned to begin when the cavalry was 70 paces from the enemy, timed the cavalry troopers approach, and ended on a long, low note intended to coincide with the moment that the charging cavalry troopers' sword struck the necks of their enemies (the phrase *de guello* refers to slitting the throat and may have been used at the battle to inform the defenders of the Alamo that no quarter would be given).

Before leaving Mexico, Santa Anna had determined that the rebelling colonists would be treated as pirates, and no quarter was given to pirates. Santa Anna had also reacted in a similar and bloody manner to rebels in several other Mexican provinces who rose in rebellion against the president's draconian rule. The President/General had enacted policies that established a strong central government and allowed the Catholic Church, wealthy land-owners, and the military to retain power and control over Mexican society. The most vocal rebellion arose in the Texas area of the Mexican state Coahuila y Tejas, and Santa Anna's decision to attack San Antonio de Béxar indicates that the true nature of his military expedition was punitive; San Antonio de Béxar was only the westernmost corner of a triangle of outposts including San Patricio, about 120 miles south of San Antonio de Béxar (northwest of present-day Corpus Christi, Texas), and La Bahía, in Goliad, about 90 miles southeast of Béxar. Militarily, the prize was Goliad, where some 500 Texian insurgents were located, but Santa Anna intended for his expedition to crush any resistance and teach the rebellious Texians a lesson.

Immediately upon entering the vicinity of the Alamo, the Mexican army began deploying troops and preparing siege works, and on the morning of February 24, the Texians awoke to find the industrious Mexicans had constructed a fortified artillery position about 400 yards west of the Alamo, where two eight-pound cannons and a howitzer were emplaced. This emplacement became known as the "River Battery." Mexican troops also began looting Texian owned property in the vicinity of the Alamo. Travis ordered all his troops and the remaining friendly civilians into the Alamo, and the defenders soon realized that the well within the Alamo grounds would not supply the water needs for the garrison. The aquecia (aqueduct) to the east of the Alamo became the alternate water source and several brief engagements occurred as Texians retrieved water. That night, the Alamo's defenders ventured on a raid outside the fort and captured a pack train of six mules and a Mexican soldier who would decipher and translate Mexican army bugle calls for the Texians until the end of the battle.

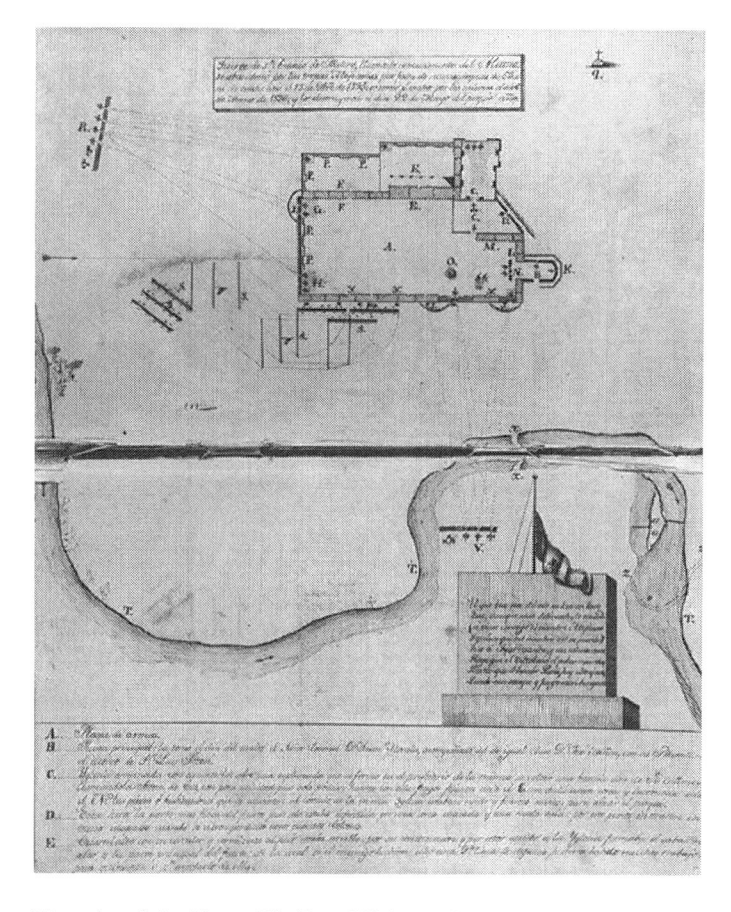

Blueprint of the Alamo. The R and V denote Mexican artillery positions

Dawn on the third day (February 25) of the siege brought unseasonably warm weather, and Santa Anna ordered an attack by 400-450 Mexican *Cazadores*, a military unit of light infantry called *Chasseurs* or "hunters" in European armies. As a rule, these types of units were used for screening and scouting before the main body of an army. In short, they were generally used to find and pinpoint enemy positions. In English, Cazadores are generally called "skirmishers." The Mexicans took cover in outlying shacks approximately 90 yards beyond the Alamo walls, and though many of the Texans assumed they were the prelude to an assault on the fort, it's now believed the Mexican soldiers had actually intended to use the huts as cover to establish an even closer artillery position.

The Mexican Cazadores approached the fort from the west, the direction of the River Battery, and probably used the concealment provided by the river's banks to screen their approach into and through the *Pueblo de Valero* (literally the "town of [the] Valero [mission]") to within fifty yards of the Alamo's walls. The *Pueblo de Valero* is likely synonymous with the long-established *Barrio del Álamo*, and both phrases likely refer to the neighborhood immediately west of the Alamo. The Texians, deploying troops in the ditches and aqueducts around the fort, eventually forced the Mexicans to retreat after two hours of fighting.

During this action, the Texians likely saw the danger of having *jacales* close to the Alamo and within their fields of fire. The term *jacal* refers to a type of small hut or shack, common throughout the American southwest and constructed of close-set, vertical poles connected with cords or sticks and with the gaps filled in with mud or adobe; this type of shelter is very similar to "waddle and daub" structures built worldwide. The *jacales* around the Alamo had served as homes for Spanish (and later Mexican) officers stationed at the Alamo and their families. Recognizing the jacales as a potential threat – the structures provided concealment to Mexican troops attempting to approach the Alamo – the Texians sent several sorties out of the fort, charged with burning the structures closest to the Alamo. As is common in Texas, the warm weather of the morning turned bitter cold in the evening, and again temperatures dropped into the 30s. Under the cover of darkness and taking advantage of the cold night, Travis sent Colonel Juan Seguín out of the fort with orders to seek assistance from General Sam Houston. The Alamo's young commander also sent out several sorties of raiders that burned additional jacales in the immediate vicinity of the Alamo. The fighting throughout that day and night was not decisive, but it proved to the Mexican force that, despite their disorganization, the Texians were able to fight when necessary.

Seguín

As the night chill fell and it became clear that the Alamo's well would not support its inhabitants, men ventured outside the wall for both water and wood, resulting in several skirmishes with Mexican pickets. By day five of the siege (February 27), the Mexican troops had exhausted their own supplies and began to "forage" for supplies in the town of Béxar. Also, having noted that the Alamo's defenders were using the eastern aqueduct as a water source, Mexican troops cut the water off at it source, eliminating a major water supply for the Alamo's defenders.

That same day, some troops from the Matamoros Battalion worked feverishly on entrenchments south of the Alamo complex, but the trenches did not meet with Santa Anna's approval, so he ordered the troops to dig new trenches closer to the Alamo's walls. Meanwhile, the Texians were digging trenches of their own, inside the "cattle pen" directly north of the old mission façade. These trench works were actually harmful to the Alamo's defense because they undermined the northern wall and forced the defenders there to expose themselves to Mexican fire whenever they moved. This last point, an observation made by Mexican officers, demonstrated one of the major weaknesses of the Alamo's defenses and a serious problem for the Texian army in general. As a rule, the Texians lacked the military training and experience which would allow them to recognize basic tactical errors (like the misplacement of a trench), and they insisted on foisting their individual rights over the appropriate practicalities of combat operations. The latter was demonstrated by the volunteers' insistence on "electing their officers."

On the Mexican side, General Antonio Gaona, traveling in the rear of the Mexican column, received orders from Santa Anna on February 27 to rapidly bring forward three battalions. Gaona complied immediately but did not bring forward any heavy siege artillery because Santa Anna had explicitly requested it. This inaction would have implications later in the battle.

As Gaona and the reinforcements moved forward on February 28, 1836 (the sixth day of the siege), news reached the Alamo that some 200 reinforcements from Goliad were en route, and morale grew among the garrison. Susannah Dickinson, the wife of Alamo defender Almeron Dickinson, reported that Crockett played a fiddle and John MacGregor (another defender) played the bagpipes in a contest of instruments. The Mexican army had received the same intelligence regarding the Goliad reinforcements, and in response, Santa Anna deployed the Jimenez Battalion and the Mexican cavalry commanded by General Ramirez y Sesma down the Goliad road to intercept the approaching Texian troops on the following day (February 29, 1836). As the blocking troops were moving into place on the Goliad road, Santa Anna proposed a three-day armistice.

In the wee hours of March 1, 1836 (the eighth day of the siege), 32 reinforcements from Gonzales arrived at the Alamo, a far cry from the 200 the defenders were still hoping to receive. The twelve-pound cannon in the Alamo fired two shots, one of which struck Santa Anna's quarters. Later in the day, General Sesma and his mixed force advanced down the Goliad road in search of the Texian reinforcements, and finding none, he returned to Béxar.

On March 2, Mexican commanders deployed troops from the Jimenez Battalion to cover a hidden road found within about 50 yards of the Alamo. Unknown to the Alamo's defenders, the provisional government, meeting at Washington-on-the-Brazos, declared Texas' Independence on this date, the ninth day of the siege. Travis ordered Lieutenant Menchaca to take a detachment of men and retrieved corn that the commander learned was stored at the Seguin Ranch. The willingness to weaken the defense to retrieve food indicates that the food supply in the Alamo was likely tenuous.

On March 3, 1836, both the Mexicans and the Alamo's defenders received what they perceived to be good news. James B. Bonham arrived at the Alamo and reported that 60 men from Gonzales were headed for the fort. Elated, the Texians fired several cannon shots into the town in celebration. That same day, Travis selected Crockett and a few other men to do some scouting in the region to try to locate a column of anticipated reinforcements under the command of Gannim. They spotted a small group of Texians camping about 20 miles away, but they were unsure whether those were Gannim's men. Historians now believe it was a mixed contingent from Gannim's aborted attempt to reinforce the Alamo and others from Gonzales. Regardless, the defenders were still outnumbered by upwards of 15-1 in early March.

Meanwhile, for the Mexicans there were two reasons for celebration. The lead elements of General Gaona's brigade arrived in Béxar, and couriers brought Santa Anna news of General Urrea's victory at San Patricio. There, on February 27, General Urrea had surprised two groups of Texian troops capturing wild horses for an assault on Matamoros (across the Rio Grande River from present-day Brownsville, Texas). The two groups were scattered and a number were killed or captured. A few of the men were able to escape capture and rejoined James Fannin at Goliad. Upon hearing news of the victory, the Mexicans rung bells throughout the town and celebrated in their camp.

Santa Anna called his officers together for a council of war on March 4, 1836. During this meeting the officers "decided" that the time for the attack would be set the following day (March 5) and that no prisoners would be taken during the assault. Above all, Santa Anna stressed the absolute necessity of the assault. One of the most controversial documents purporting to be an account of the Alamo was the diary of the Texas campaign by José Enrique de la Peña, and historians still debate whether it was a forgery or authentic. In his diary, de la Peña reported that the officers present at the council, "Generals Sesma, Cos, and Castrillón, [and] Colonels Almonte, Duque, Amat, Romero, and Salas," knew their commander and his refusal to accept any opposition. De la Peña, a Lieutenant Colonel, further reported that some of them agreed with Santa Anna when he was present, only to disagree with the General/President in his absence. Additionally, some Mexican officers felt that the attack was completely unnecessary, including de la Peña and Captain José Juan Sánchez Navarro y Estrada, who wrote in his journal that Santa Anna favored his victories "to be marked by blood and tears!" The de la Peña diary also documented the disapproval General Castrillón and Colonel Almonte held for Santa Anna's decision to execute any and all survivors of the coming battle (Santa Anna later modified this order to spare women present in the Alamo). In addition, de la Peña's narrative recorded Castríllon and Almonte's protest when Santa Anna prepared to execute the prisoner taken by General Urrea at San Patricio stating that the men cited the "the rights of men, [and] philosophical and humane principles which did them honor." However, the officers' protestations had no effect on Santa Anna's decision.

That same evening Bowie's cousin-in-law Juana Navarro Alsbury came forth asking once again to negotiate a surrender for the garrison. Already impatient, Santa Anna rejected the overture, and some believe that Alsbury's appearance only encouraged him to move the assault up from March 7 to March 6

The Alamo's defenders found themselves in a desperate position. Their major source of water had been cut-off, they were only receiving small numbers of reinforcements, and their food supplies and ammunition were running short. The Mexican bombardment was having the desired effect, and many Mexican officers felt that the Alamo's defenders would soon surrender, which would certainly result in the least casualties for the Mexicans as well. But the real reason for the Texas campaign, and the Béxar campaign in particular, was not to secure the Texians' surrender; its purpose was to avenge General Cos's defeat at San Antonio de Béxar in December 1835, and to destroy the Texas Revolt. Meanwhile, the Alamo's defenders insisted on holding out despite the fact that their superiors didn't believe the defense of the compound was necessary and had ordered it destroyed just weeks earlier. Thus, the stage was set for Santa Anna's vengeance to be inflicted upon the Texians in the Alamo.

Late in the evening, the Alamo received another group of reinforcements, possibly the 60 men Bonham had reported were en route from Gonzales. They would be the last reinforcements the Alamo received. The defenders also discovered that the Mexicans' artillery had been combined into two large emplacements within about 200 yards of the fort, despite being under near constant fire from the Texians.

On March 5, Santa Anna was now certain that the attack would take place in the pre-dawn hours of March 6 and ordered Mexican troops to begin reconnaissance sorties around the fort to determine the most advantageous routes of approach. The Mexican commander appointed Generals Cos and Colonels Duque, Romero, and Morales to lead each of four attacking columns. The columns under Cos and Duque totaled about 700 troops, and Cos would assault the western wall while Duque would attack the north. Colonel Romero's column was composed of about 300 fusiliers, and they were ordered to attack the east side of the fort. Finally, Colonel Morales and a force of over 100 Cazadores were charged with taking the entrenchments guarding the fort's entrance and the entrance itself. Some 400 troops, the Sapper Battalion (commanded by Santa Anna himself) and five grenadier companies, were held in reserve. The troops manning blocking positions would be recalled after dark, and all the Mexican soldiers would turn in to sleep at dark to be ready to move into position at midnight. Ladders had been prepared, and the troops were ordered to carry hatchets and crowbars with them to help overcome the fort's defenses.

According to legend and oral accounts by Susanna Dickinson, one of the only Texians to survive the coming battle, Travis assembled the defenders on March 5 to let them know that an attack was certainly imminent. Dickinson claimed that Travis drew a line in the sand and asked those who would fight to cross the line and stand with him, which all but one man did. While the story that Travis literally drew a line in the sand has been largely discounted among historians, they agree that he did give the defenders the chance to stay and die in the fight or leave with their lives. The day before the culminating battle, George Allen was dispatched as a courier, indicating that even at this late date, the garrison could have withdrawn. In his diary entry for March 5, Crockett wrote down, "Pop, pop, pop! Bom, bom, bom! throughout the day. No time for memorandums now. Go ahead! Liberty and Independence forever."

Dickinson

The Battle of the Alamo

Santa Anna shrewdly stopped the bombardment at about 10:00 p.m. on the night of March 5, letting the weary defenders fall deeply asleep for the first time since the siege started. At midnight, Mexican troops moved to staging areas and awaited the order to attack.

At about 5:30 AM, the order to attack came and the Mexican troops quietly began to advance. They first encountered sleeping, Texian sentries and killed them as they slept, but the excitement of the battle overcame the silent Mexican troops as they advanced, and calls of "Viva la

Republica!" and "Viva Santa Anna!" began to ring out in the early morning dark.

Adjutant John Baugh, making early morning rounds in the Alamo, was surprised by the Mexican shouts and rushed to awaken Travis. The Alamo's commander and his slave Joe grabbed their weapons and rushed to the north battery, rousing men and shouting as he went. Unsure of the enemy's disposition, the Alamo's gunners fired their cannons blindly, and the muzzle flash revealed the dire nature of their predicament; the Mexicans had nearly reached the walls of the fort.

The Texians' cannons, loaded with metal scraps, chain, and shot, tore huge gaps in the lines of advancing Mexican troops and the cries of the dead and dying filled the darkness. While the Texans on the wall were firing at the massed Mexican column advancing, the Mexicans in back started wildly firing, doing more damage via friendly fire to other Mexicans than defenders. Among the first to arrive at the wall, Travis fired his shotgun down at the approaching troops, and as he reloaded he was struck by a single ball in the forehead and slumped over dead. Of all the confusion, chaos and controversy that was about to ensue, it is universally agreed that Travis was among the first of the defenders to die. His death also demonstrated that there were too many advancing Mexicans for the Texians to take the time out to reload their guns, an important lesson that the Texian defenders were about to learn all across their defensive lines.

The Alamo's cannon fire greatly reduced the numbers of Mexican troops, and its deadliness and ferocity forced three of the Mexican columns (Cos, Duque, and Romero) to converge at the base of the north wall. Colonel Duque was injured and General Castrillón relieved him and assumed command of his column. The Mexican attack had stalled, and fearing a disaster, Santa Anna committed the reserve troops. Meanwhile, Cos ordered his column to wheel right, and the soldiers attacked the west wall, using axes and crowbars to break through barricaded windows and other openings. Soon, Mexican troops were pouring through gun ports and climbing over the wall to gain entry into the Alamo.

Colonel Morales and about 100 troops attacked what they thought was a weakness in the wall, but they were quickly repelled by withering fire from Davy Crockett, his volunteers, and a single cannon. The Mexican troops turned toward the southwest corner of the Alamo and sought cover behind an old stone building and the remains of burned jacales. Meanwhile, General Amador and the reserve force scrambled up the rough repairs in the north wall made by the Texians and soon breached the wall, allowing the Mexican to flood into the fort. In response to the north wall breach, the Texians shifted cannon fire to cover the area. Now sensing his opportunity, Colonel Morales and his men stormed the southwest corner, taking the eighteen-pounder cannon and the fort's main entrance. The fort was now largely open to the Mexican assault.

In a room near the Alamo's main entrance, Mexican troops found Bowie, ill and in bed. Some claim that he was taken alive from his room, others claim he committed suicide, and the most likely account is that Bowie propped himself up in his bed, waited for the Mexicans to arrive, and then took aim and maybe even used his famous Bowie knife if the enemy got within range. Naturally, the most popular version was that he was found dead, a pistol in one hand and his famous Bowie knife in the other, surrounded by dozens of dead Mexican soldiers. Regardless of whether he offered resistance, was taken alive, or killed in his room, Bowie would soon be dead.

Seeing Mexican troops pouring into the Alamo from all sides, the Texians turned their cannons on the advancing troops, devastating their ranks, but the Mexican troops continued to advance. With wholesale breaches of the wall, the Texian defenders now began to fall back as planned to rooms in the Long Barracks that had been fortified in advance with trenches and barricades made of rawhide filled with earth. It is believed Crockett and some of the men under his command were among the last defenders who were out in the open, and they engaged in hand-to-hand fighting before some of the remaining defenders made their way into the church.

In their haste to retreat, the defenders had failed to spike their cannons. The Mexican troops moved from room to room, clearing each with swords, bayonets, and knives, but eventually the enraged Mexicans turned the Texian cannons on the fortified rooms. Eventually, the only resistance was coming from the church, and again, the Mexican troops used the Texian cannons against the last of the defenders. Robert Evans, the ordnance chief, attempted near the end to detonate the entire powder magazine in the barracks, which would have blown up the barracks and the chapel and taken not just a number of the Mexicans but also the women and children still in the church. He was shot and killed by a musket ball with his torch just inches away from the store of powder.

As the Mexicans finally killed every defender in the barracks, the last resistance came from about a dozen men manning the two 12-pounder cannon in the chapel. One of the last to die was a young boy, the son of Texian Anthony Wolf, who pulled a blanket over his shoulders as the Mexicans approached the sacristy of the church. Mistaking him for a soldier, the advancing Mexicans shot him.

With the last resisters quelled, Mexican soldiers walked around bayoneting any body that was still moving until they had verified that all of the Alamo's defenders were dead. In the confusion, more instances of friendly fire added to the Mexican casualty count even as none of their enemy remained. Accounts agree that about half a dozen defenders were captured, and according to to de la Peña, one of them was Davy Crockett. As these prisoners were brought before Santa Anna, General Castrillón petitioned the Mexican commander for mercy on their behalves, but the President/General only answered with a gesture of indignation and ordered the prisoners executed. According to de la Peña, some officers who near the President, probably wishing to impress him, immediately drew swords and executed the prisoners. The battle was over and all of the Alamo's defenders were now dead.

Aftermath of the Battle

While the facts surrounding the Battle of the Alamo continue to be debated, there is no doubt what that battle has come to symbolize. Santa Anna believed that spreading news of the battle would induce the remaining armies, still outnumbered about 6-1 by the Mexicans, to quit the fight. Instead, the Alamo became the ultimate rallying cry for those seeking independence. Instead of considering the defense futile and needless, Americans have instead chosen to "Remember the Alamo" as a heroic struggle against impossible odds, and the Alamo is viewed as a place where men took a stand and made the ultimate sacrifice in the name of freedom. For this reason, the Alamo remains hallowed ground and the "Shrine of Texas Liberty".

Naturally, as the three most famous defenders at the Alamo, Travis, Crockett and Bowie have continued to fascinate Americans, and there is still controversy over the deaths of Bowie and Crockett. Crockett's death is the most contentious. Weeks after the Battle of Fort Alamo, stories began to circulate that Davy Crockett was among those who surrendered and was subsequently executed by firing squad or sword. A former slave known as "Ben," however, who acted as cook for one of Santa Anna's officers, maintained to his death that Davy's body was found in the barracks surrounded by "no less than sixteen Mexican corpses," with Crockett's knife buried in one of them. Susannah Dickinson claimed she saw his body near the entry to the barracks, suggesting he had died while still fighting out in the open.

On the other end of the spectrum, there were accusations that in an act of cowardice, he had himself locked up in the mission jail and pretended to be a prisoner of the garrison. Both Ben's version and the cowardice charge are almost certainly untrue, as is the even more unbelievable suggestion that he somehow escaped prior to the pre-dawn assault. Most historians believe Crockett was killed in the fighting, pointing to the fact that accounts that claim he was executed may have been fabricated for propaganda purposes intending to rile up the locals against the Mexicans.

Whether one believes Crockett died while fighting or was part of the group who surrendered and was summarily executed mostly depends on whether they believe de la Peña's diary is authentic. According to author Mary Petite, "every account of the Crockett surrender-execution story comes from an avowed antagonist (either on political or military grounds) of Santa Anna's. It is believed that many stories, such as the surrender and execution of Crockett, were created and spread in order to discredit Santa Anna and add to his role as villain."

Chapter 9: Crockett's Legacy

Author

In 1834, two years before his death, Davy Crockett enlisted the help of Kentucky State Representative Thomas Chilton to help write his memoirs, aptly titled *A Narrative of the Life of David Crockett* (also appearing as *The Autobiography of David Crockett*). Although most historians consider what resulted a clever melding of fact and fantasy, the work is credited with introducing a new genre of spirited, realistic writing into American literature.

While other works are often attributed to Davy (though presumed actually penned by ghost writers due his lack of formal education), perhaps most notable is "Bear Hunting in Tennessee," a story from *A Narrative of the Life of David Crockett*. This excerpt (much of which appeared in an earlier part of this book) emphasized Crockett's reputation as a great bear hunter and one of the first "mighty hunters" in the "Southwestern humor" literary genre. It was clearly crafted to further the myth that allowed Davy to become a legend of the frontier within his lifetime and continue to be so for years to come. By the time of his death, it was widely believed that Davy had actually killed a bear when he was only three years old.

The Crockett Almanack (*Davy Crockett's Almanack of Wild Sports in the West, Crockett's Yaller Flower Almanack*) was published for many years after his death. Produced by "Boon Crockett," among others, it capitalized on Davy's famous adventures, with many of the tales attributed to Davy's own narrative. The Daughters of the Republic of Texas Library at the Alamo say that at least 45 such almanacs were published between 1835 and 1856.

Homage

In 1853, the name-sake clipper ship, "the Crockett," was launched in Connecticut, gaining great popularity over the next 40 years sailing from New York to San Francisco, and New York to Liverpool, England.

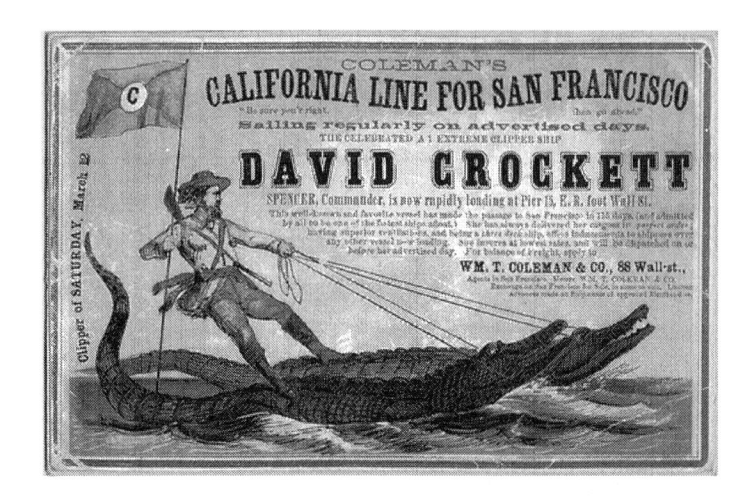

From 1872-1896, the Frank Murdock/Frank Mayo play *Davy Crockett; or, Be Sure Then Go Ahead* (with Mayo in the title role) toured the U. S. (until Mayo died).

In 1903, the military facility on Galveston Island, Texas (established in the late 1890s) was named "Fort Crockett" in Davy's honor, as an acknowledgment of his heroism at the Battle of the Alamo.

Crockett, a city in Houston County, Texas, was named after Davy Crockett, who reportedly camped nearby while *en route* to the Alamo. The site is very near the Old San Antonio Road.

Crockett County, located in Tennessee and formed in 1871 from portions of Haywood, Madison, Dyer, and Gibson counties, was named in honor of David Crockett. Its capital city is Alamo.

The section of U. S. Route 64 between Winchester, Tennessee and Lawrenceburg, Tennessee is named the David Crockett Memorial Highway.

The M28 Davy Crockett Weapon System is a small nuclear weapons system (the smallest developed by the U. S.) that can be fired from a light vehicle, or even from a shoulder-mounted launcher. In keeping with Crockett*esque* humor, the rocket is said to be able to "take out more than just b'ars -- it can take out the whole forest!"

A replica of his birthplace cabin now stands near the original site in eastern Tennessee (in what is now Greene County, Tennessee) in Davy Crockett Birthplace State Park.

On the site where Davy's father built a tavern in the early 1790s, a museum now stands, believed to be a faithful reconstruction of the original.

The definitive painting of the Alamo battle, *The Fall of the Alamo*, by American artist Robert Jenkins Onderdonk (1852-1917), depicts Davy Crockett swinging his rifle at Mexican troops who have breached the south gate of the mission.

A coffin in the San Fernando Cathedral in downtown San Antonio, Texas, purports to hold the ashes of the Alamo defenders. Historians, however, believe it more probable that the ashes were buried near the Alamo due to an enduring oral account that contends that once all of the defenders had been killed, Santa Anna ordered his men to take the bodies to a nearby stand of trees where they were stacked together, wood was piled on top and then set on fire.

The ashes are said to have been left undisturbed until February 1837 when Juan Seguin (a 19th-century Texas Senator, Mayor, Judge, and Justice of the Peace who played prominently in the Texas Revolution) returned to Bexar [San Antonio de Béxar] to examine the remains. Legend contends that a local carpenter created a simple coffin where the ashes from the funeral pyres were placed and the names of Travis, Crockett, and Bowie inscribed on the lid. Thought to have been buried in a peach grove, the spot where the coffin is believed buried was not marked, and therefore no longer identifiable. Many historians discredit this account and believe that Crockett and the other defenders received no such honorable treatment.

Frontiersman, Militiaman, Congressman, Defender

"Born on a mountain top in Tennessee
The greenest state in the land of the free
Raised in the woods so's he knew ev'ry tree
Kilt him a b'ar when he was only three
Davy, Davy Crockett, king of the wild frontier
Fought single-handed through many a war
Till the enemy was whipped and peace was in store
And while he was handlin' this risky chore
He made himself a legend forever more
Davy, Davy Crockett, the man who knew no fear" - Tom W. Blackburn, "The Ballad of Davy Crockett" (1955)

Few names in American history evoke the same imagery as Davy Crockett. Iconic in representing the American pioneering spirit, he was a famous frontiersman (expert trapper, marksman, and backwoodsman), colonel in the Tennessee militia, and served as a Congressman, proving to be a rare breed of statesman, indeed. But, what else is really *known* about him?

Ultimately, that's a question surrounded by great speculation.

In many regards, Crockett can be considered among the greatest self-promoters in the history of the United States. Known as one of the greatest adventurers of his time, the fame that spread early in his life was as much a matter of his legendary exploits as the "yarns," "tall tales," and myths he perpetuated, which most who met him could not differentiate.

Charismatic and possessing a mastery of vernacular that made him a natural storyteller, it seems likely that he created and promoted the legends that invariably preceded him and which he would then subsequently confirm, of course. As a result, the legend of an "eccentric but shrewd b'ar-hunting, Indian-fighting frontiersman" grew, with biographers like Thomas Chilton (co-author of his *Narrative*) helping to feed the growing myth.

Fully aware of his mounting celebrity, Davy wrote: "I know, that obscure as I am, my name is making a considerable deal of fuss in the world. I can't tell why it is, nor in what it is to end. Go where I will, everybody seems anxious to get a peep at me; and it would be hard to tell which would have the advantage, if I, and the "Government," and "Black Hawk," and a great eternal big caravan of wild varments were all to be showed at the same time in four different parts of any of the big cities in the nation. I am not so sure that I shouldn't get the most custom of any of the crew. There must therefore be something in me, or about me, that attracts attention, which is even mysterious to myself. I can't understand it, and I therefore put all the facts down, leaving the reader free to take his choice of them."[21]

A Man of Humor

Like other "yarn spinners" of the time, men who told far-fetched stories to entertain family and friends, Davy Crockett was known as a "humorist." Much like Mark Twain or James MacGillivray, such men were expected to exaggerate the facts of a story and embellish the setting, characters and storyline to mythical proportions, which would certainly make the story more entertaining. And at the same time, no one was expected to believe the tall tale as fact.

But unlike Twain and MacGillivray, Crockett's tales usually focused around himself. One often- repeated story tells of him cornering a raccoon in a tree, and as he took aim at the animal with his famous rifle "Betsy", it recognized his opponent and quickly acknowledged the futility of trying to escape, crying, "Don't shoot, Colonel! I'll come down! I know when I'm a gone coon!" The story is clearly a literary vehicle used to convey his marksmanship skills and the wide range of his fame.

---

[21] Project Gutenberg eBook, "A Narrative of the Life of David Crockett, of the State of Tennessee, by Davy Crockett." [7]

Crockett Quotes

Davy is said to have greeted a crowd while campaigning for Congress, bragging, "I'm that same David Crockett, fresh from the backwoods, half-horse, half-alligator, a little touched of the snapping turtle; can wade the Mississippi, leap the Ohio, ride upon a streak of lightning, and slip without a scratch down a honey locust [tree]."

One of Davy's most repeated adages (published in *Crockett's Almanac*) is: "Always be sure you are right, then go ahead."

Others include, "In one word I'm a screamer, and have got the roughest racking horse, the prettiest sister, the surest rifle and the ugliest dog in the district"; "My father can whip any man in Kentucky, and I can lick my father"; and "I can run faster, dive deeper, stay longer under, and come out drier, than any chap this side the big Swamp. I can outlook a panther and out-stare a flash of lightning, tote a steamboat on my back and play at rough and tumble with a lion, and an occasional kick from a zebra."

Kilt Him a B'ar

One of the most enduring "Davy-identifiable" tales surrounding the legendary backwoodsman describes his encounter and subsequent victory over a black bear "when he was only three."

While it is historically verifiable that hunters of his day hunted bear for meat and fur (coats), we have only Davy's own account of his hunting exploits, which can be considered great exaggeration (and perhaps even fabrication.) Although Davy himself thought it stretching the truth too far to claim super-human strength and wherewithal at age three, he nonetheless claimed to have killed one hundred five bears in one seven-month hunting season alone (1825-1826), bringing forty-seven to their demise in a single month. Among his many enlivened tales, he describes an encounter on a "moonless night in January" when he found himself locked in mortal combat with a fully-grown black bear, writing, "I made a lounge [sic] with my long knife, and fortunately, stuck him right in the heart."[22] As is always the case, however, Davy's imaginative accounts must be taken with a proverbial *grain of salt*.

La Rebelión de Texas

In 1955, Jesús Sánchez Garza self-published a book he titled *La Rebelión de Texas— Manuscrito Inédito de 1836 por un Ofical de Santa Anna*, purported to be the memoirs of one José Enrique de la Peña, a Mexican officer present at the Battle of the Alamo.

---

[22] Wallis, Michael. *David Crockett: The Lion of the West*. Page 7.

In 1975, Texas A&M University Press published an English translation of the book, calling it, *With Santa Anna in Texas: A Personal Narrative of the Revolution.* Upon its release, the English version ignited renewed controversy, as it alleged that Davy Crockett did not die in battle. Because the original book was self-published, and no publisher ever verified the authenticity or surce of its content, historians disagree on whether aspects of the book were falsified or even completely fabricated. Adding to the tenuous nature of the authority of the book is the fact that Garza never explained how he gained access to de la Peña's personal documents after his death.

Some historians, including Bill Groneman, found it suspicious that Garza's compilation was published in 1955, just at the height of interest in Crockett and the Alamo ignited by Walt Disney's television miniseries about Crockett's life, *Davy Crockett*. Groneman also points out that the de la Peña journals are made up of several different types of paper from several different paper manufacturers, all cut down to fit, suggesting fraud.

However, Professor of History James Crisp from North Carolina State University, has studied the documents and is convinced they are genuine. Additionally, in October of 2001, in a *Southwestern Historical Quarterly* article, Dr. David B. Gracy II of the University of Texas at Austin, attested to the authenticity of de la Pena's work. Thus, the debate has only intensified. The original manuscript, consisting of 200 loose pages, was auctioned in 1998 for $387,500 and now resides at the "Center for American History" at the University of Texas at Austin.

No other accounts of Crockett surviving the Alamo have surfaced besides de la Peña's diary, and no documentation in the archives of the Mexican government nor any of the personal records of others present at the Battle of the Alamo reference survivors among the defenders.

Perspective

Though a consummate self-promoter who continually sold his folksy persona by encouraging the informal "Davy" to everyone he met, he always signed his name "David." And while his childhood exploits and natural talents for hunting and trapping were undoubtedly formidable—perhaps extraordinary by frontier standards—in reality, it was urban legend, dime-store novels, and Hollywood that produced and perpetuated the *Huck Finn-like-character-turned-frontiersman-turn-statesman* Americans know him as today. Even his legendary coonskin cap was more of a prop (then and in lore) that he held in his hand more than he wore on his head. Not unlike other *larger-than-life* folk heroes of the American West (like Daniel Boone), figures who embodied frontier vitality and determination, Davy ultimately became a mere caricature of his true self (whoever that may have been).

By the late 19th century, Davy Crockett and his seemingly indomitable legend had actually become largely forgotten. In fact, many Americans had come to accept that Davy Crockett and Daniel Boone were actually fictional characters. But on December 15, 1954, the legend was reborn when Walt Disney aired the first of a three-episode series called *Davy Crockett, Indian Fighter*, starring Fess Parker as "Davy". It was part of a promotional campaign tied to building the theme park *Disneyland* in Anaheim, California (dedicated on July 17, 1955).

Literally overnight, "Davy Crockett" frenzy swept across the country, and by the end of the three-episode run Crockett had once again become the most famous frontiersman in American history. But the show was not without controversy. Juxtaposed to the new-found interest, a heated debate erupted, with viewers questioning whether Davy the actual historic figure really deserved the amount of attention he was now receiving. Other letter writers questioned the series' historical accuracy. But despite a largely fictionalized and certainly glamorized account of his life and times, the series proved extraordinarily popular, and they were subsequently cobbled into a feature-length movie in the summer of 1955 with Fess Parker and side-kick Buddy Ebsen (of *Beverly Hillbillies* fame) touring the U. S., Europe, and Japan, enlivening the characters before adoring crowds. By the end of 1955, Americans had purchased over $300 million worth of Davy Crockett merchandise, and over $2 billion by 2001.

The television series also introduced the popular song, "The Ballad of Davy Crockett," with four different versions of the tune hitting the *Billboard Best Sellers* pop chart in 1955. The versions sung by Bill Hayes, TV series star Fess Parker, and legendary contemporary singer Tennessee Ernie Ford charted in the Top 10 simultaneously, with Hayes' version hitting #1.

In the 1960s, the original shows were repeated on the NBC Television Network (after Disney moved his programming to that network), marking the first time the programs were shown in color. Davy then starred in two further Disney adventures, "Davy Crockett's Keelboat Race" and "Davy Crockett and the River Pirates." Then two decades later, in the 1988–1989 television season, a three-episode revival was made entitled *The New Adventures of Davy Crockett*, in which Tim Dunigan assumed Fess Parker's famous role. Legendary Country/Rock-a-Billy singer Johnny Cash played an older Davy in a few scenes set before he went to Texas.

Though the fad eventually ran its course, Davy Crockett was always a prominent role in film accounts about the Alamo, the most famous of which was John Wayne's *The Alamo*. In addition to directing it and producing an unabashed movie meant to be patriotic, Wayne starred as Crockett. At one point, Wayne's Crockett exhorts, "Republic. I like the sound of the word. Means that people can live free, talk free, go or come, buy or sell, be drunk or sober, however they choose. Some words give you a feeling. Republic is one of those words that makes me tight in the throat." When Wayne himself was asked about what statement he was trying to make in *The Alamo*, he responded, "I thought it would be a tremendous epic picture that would say 'America.'"

Virtually since the invention of movie-making, Davy Crockett has been a popular role. On film, Davy has been brought to life by:

    Charles K. French (*Hearts United*, 1909, silent film)
    Dustin Farnum (*Davy Crockett*, 1916, silent film)
    Cullen Landis (*Davy Crockett at the Fall of the Alamo*, 1926, silent film)
    Jack Perrin (*The Painted Stallion*, 1937)
    Lane Chandler (*Heroes of the Alamo*, 1937)
    Robert Barrat (*Man of Conquest*, 1939)
    George Montgomery (as Davy Crockett, cousin of the *famous* Davy Crockett, *Indian Scout*, 1950)
    Trevor Bardette (*The Man From the Alamo*, 1953)
    Arthur Hunnicutt (*The Last Command*, 1955)
    Fess Parker (with Buddy Ebsen, *Davy Crockett, King of the Wild Frontier,* 1955; and *Davy Crockett and the River Pirates*, 1956)
    James Griffith (*The First Texan*, 1956)
    John Wayne (*The Alamo*, 1960)
    Brian Keith (*The Alamo: Thirteen Days to Glory*, 1987)
    Merrill Connally (*Alamo: The Price of Freedom*, 1988)
    Johnny Cash (*Davy Crockett: Rainbow in the Thunder*, 1988)
    Tim Dunigan (*Davy Crockett: Rainbow in the Thunder; Davy Crockett: A Natural Man; Davy Crockett: Guardian Spirit; Davy Crockett: Letter to Polly*, 1988–1989)
    David Zucker (an homage in *The Naked Gun 2½: The Smell of Fear*, 1991)
    John Schneider (*Texas*, 1994)
    Scott Wickware (*Dear America: A Line in the Sand*, 2000)
    Justin Howard (*The Anarchist Cookbook*, 2002)
    Billy Bob Thornton (*The Alamo*, 2004)

In recent years, a seventh-season episode of the *Discovery Channel* series "Myth Busters" explored one story of Crockett's legendary backwoods exploits: that he could wedge an axe into a tree trunk and then fire his long rifle from forty yards and hit the edge so precisely that the bullet would split in two. After some practice, marksman Tory Belleci was able to duplicate the feat from twenty yards with the gun resting on sandbags, thus declaring the myth "Confirmed." Of course, as with seemingly everything else about his life, the fact that Crockett could have done it doesn't mean that he actually did.

The Not Yours to Give Speech

The Not Yours to Give speech is a classic example of the Davy Crockett legend, in which an apocryphal speech or story is credited to the frontiersman to help others score political points. In this case, Crockett is credited with giving a conservative speech that even people today cite as being against welfare and the use of government spending of taxpayer money.

In an 1884 "dime" novel written by Edward S. Ellis titled *The Life of Colonel David Crockett*, Davy Crockett is described as giving a speech criticizing his fellow Congressmen for spending taxpayer dollars to help the widow of a U. S. Navy man without contributing some of their own salary to the cause. Ellis describes how the once-popular proposal died in Congress largely due to Crockett's impassioned speech.

However, the authenticity of the speech has been rejected by Crockett biographer Jim Boylston, who noted several inconsistencies in an article published in 2004, including the facts that the *Register of Debates* (the record of the Congressional debates of the 18th Congress, 2nd Session through the 25th Congress, 1st Session, 1824--1837) and the *Congressional Globe* (the record of the Congressional debates of the 23rd through 42nd Congresses, 1833--1873) do not contain transcripts of speeches made on the House floor, where the speech would have taken place. Boylston, who has published about Crockett's time spent in Congress, concluded that Crockett likely never gave the speech (and further points out that Crockett frequently appropriated government money to help individuals in his district).

Regardless, here is how Ellis described the story and speech:

One day in the House of Representatives, a bill was taken up appropriating money for the benefit of a widow of a distinguished naval officer. Several beautiful speeches had been made in its support. The Speaker was just about to put the question when Crockett arose:

"Mr. Speaker–I have as much respect for the memory of the deceased, and as much sympathy for the sufferings of the living, if suffering there be, as any man in this House, but we must not permit our respect for the dead or our sympathy for a part of the living to lead us into an act of injustice to the balance of the living. I will not go into an argument to prove that Congress has no power to appropriate this money as an act of charity. Every member upon this floor knows it. We have the right, as individuals, to give away as much of our own money as we please in charity; but as members of Congress we have no right so to appropriate a dollar of the public money. Some eloquent appeals have been made to us upon the ground that it is a debt due the deceased. Mr. Speaker, the deceased lived long after the close of the war; he was in office to the day of his death, and I have never heard that the government was in arrears to him.

Every man in this House knows it is not a debt. We cannot, without the grossest corruption, appropriate this money as the payment of a debt. We have not the semblance of authority to appropriate it as a charity. Mr. Speaker, I have said we have the right to give as much money of our own as we please. I am the poorest man on this floor. I cannot vote for this bill, but I will give one week's pay to the object, and if every member of Congress will do the same, it will amount to more than the bill asks."

He took his seat. Nobody replied. The bill was put upon its passage, and, instead of passing unanimously, as was generally supposed, and as, no doubt, it would, but for that speech, it received but few votes, and, of course, was lost.

Later, when asked by a friend why he had opposed the appropriation, Crockett gave this explanation:

"Several years ago I was one evening standing on the steps of the Capitol with some other members of Congress, when our attention was attracted by a great light over in Georgetown . It was evidently a large fire. We jumped into a hack and drove over as fast as we could. In spite of all that could be done, many houses were burned and many families made homeless, and, besides, some of them had lost all but the clothes they had on. The weather was very cold, and when I saw so many women and children suffering, I felt that something ought to be done for them. The next morning a bill was introduced appropriating $20,000 for their relief. We put aside all other business and rushed it through as soon as it could be done.

"The next summer, when it began to be time to think about the election, I concluded I would take a scout around among the boys of my district. I had no opposition there, but, as the election was some time off, I did not know what might turn up. When riding one day in a part of my district in which I was more of a stranger than any other, I saw a man in a field plowing and coming toward the road. I gauged my gait so that we should meet as he came to the fence. As he came up, I spoke to the man. He replied politely, but, as I thought, rather coldly.

"I began: 'Well, friend, I am one of those unfortunate beings called candidates, and–'

"'Yes, I know you; you are Colonel Crockett, I have seen you once before, and voted for you the last time you were elected. I suppose you are out electioneering now, but you had better not waste your time or mine. I shall not vote for you again.'

"This was a sockdolager . . . I begged him to tell me what was the matter.

"'Well, Colonel, it is hardly worth-while to waste time or words upon it. I do not see how it can be mended, but you gave a vote last winter which shows that either you have not capacity to understand the Constitution, or that you are wanting in the honesty and firmness to be guided by it. In either case you are not the man to represent me. But I beg your pardon for expressing it in that way. I did not intend to avail myself of the privilege of the constituent to speak plainly to a candidate for the purpose of insulting or wounding you. I intend by it only to say that your understanding of the Constitution is very different from mine; and I will say to you what, but for my rudeness, I should not have said, that I believe you to be honest. . . . But an understanding of the Constitution different from mine I cannot overlook, because the Constitution, to be worth anything, must be held sacred, and rigidly observed in all its provisions. The man who wields power and misinterprets it is the more dangerous the more honest he is.'

"'I admit the truth of all you say, but there must be some mistake about it, for I do not remember that I gave any vote last winter upon any constitutional question.'

"'No, Colonel, there's no mistake. Though I live here in the backwoods and seldom go from home, I take the papers from Washington and read very carefully all the proceedings of Congress. My papers say that last winter you voted for a bill to appropriate $20,000 to some sufferers by a fire in Georgetown . Is that true?'

"'Well, my friend; I may as well own up. You have got me there. But certainly nobody will complain that a great and rich country like ours should give the insignificant sum of $20,000 to relieve its suffering women and children, particularly with a full and overflowing Treasury, and I am sure, if you had been there, you would have done just as I did.'

"'It is not the amount, Colonel, that I complain of; it is the principle. In the first place, the government ought to have in the Treasury no more than enough for its legitimate purposes. But that has nothing to do with the question. The power of collecting and disbursing money at pleasure is the most dangerous power that can be intrusted to man, particularly under our system of collecting revenue by a tariff, which reaches every man in the country, no matter how poor he may be, and the poorer he is the more he pays in proportion to his means. What is worse, it presses upon him without his knowledge where the weight centers, for there is not a man in the United States who can ever guess how much he pays to the government. So you see, that while you are contributing to relieve one, you are drawing it from thousands who are even worse off than he. If you had the right to give anything, the amount was simply a matter of discretion with you, and you had as much right to give $20,000,000 as $20,000. If you have the right to give to one, you have the right to give to all; and, as the Constitution neither defines charity nor stipulates the amount, you are at liberty to give to any and everything which you may believe, or profess to believe, is a charity, and to any amount you may think proper. You will very easily perceive what a wide door this would open for fraud and corruption and favoritism, on the one hand, and for robbing the people on the other. No, Colonel, Congress has no right to give charity. Individual members may give as much of their own money as they please, but they have no right to touch a dollar of the public money for that purpose. If twice as many houses had been burned in this county as in Georgetown , neither you nor any other member of Congress would have thought of appropriating a dollar for our relief. There are about two hundred and forty members of Congress. If they had shown their sympathy for the sufferers by contributing each one week's pay, it would have made over $13,000. There are plenty of wealthy men in and around Washington who could have given $20,000 without depriving themselves of even a luxury of life. The congressmen chose to keep their own money, which, if reports be true, some of them spend not very creditably; and the people about Washington , no doubt, applauded you for relieving them from the necessity of giving by giving what was not yours to give. The people have delegated to Congress, by the Constitution, the power to do certain things. To do these, it is authorized to collect and pay moneys, and for nothing else. Everything beyond this is usurpation, and a violation of the Constitution.

"'So you see, Colonel, you have violated the Constitution in what I consider a vital point. It is a precedent fraught with danger to the country, for when Congress once begins to stretch its power beyond the limits of the Constitution, there is no limit to it, and no security for the people. I have no doubt you acted honestly, but that does not make it any better, except as far as you are personally concerned, and you see that I cannot vote for you.'

"I tell you I felt streaked. I saw if I should have opposition, and this man should go to talking, he would set others to talking, and in that district I was a gone fawn-skin. I could not answer him, and the fact is, I was so fully convinced that he was right, I did not want to. But I must satisfy him, and I said to him:

"'Well, my friend, you hit the nail upon the head when you said I had not sense enough to understand the Constitution. I intended to be guided by it, and thought I had studied it fully. I have heard many speeches in Congress about the powers of Congress, but what you have said here at your plow has got more hard, sound sense in it than all the fine speeches I ever heard. If I had ever taken the view of it that you have, I would have put my head into the fire before I would have given that vote; and if you will forgive me and vote for me again, if I ever vote for another unconstitutional law I wish I may be shot.'

"He laughingly replied: 'Yes, Colonel, you have sworn to that once before, but I will trust you again upon one condition. You say that you are convinced that your vote was wrong. Your acknowledgment of it will do more good than beating you for it. If, as you go around the district, you will tell people about this vote, and that you are satisfied it was wrong, I will not only vote for you, but will do what I can to keep down opposition, and, perhaps, I may exert some little influence in that way.'

"'If I don't,' said I, 'I wish I may be shot; and to convince you that I am in earnest in what I say I will come back this way in a week or ten days, and if you will get up a gathering of the people, I will make a speech to them. Get up a barbecue, and I will pay for it.'

"'No, Colonel, we are not rich people in this section, but we have plenty of provisions to contribute for a barbecue, and some to spare for those who have none. The push of crops will be over in a few days, and we can then afford a day for a barbecue. This is Thursday; I will see to getting it up on Saturday week. Come to my house on Friday, and we will go together, and I promise you a very respectable crowd to see and hear you.'

"'Well, I will be here. But one thing more before I say good-by. I must know your name.'

"'My name is Bunce.'

"'Not Horatio Bunce?'

"'Yes.'

"'Well, Mr. Bunce, I never saw you before, though you say you have seen me, but I know you very well. I am glad I have met you, and very proud that I may hope to have you for my friend.'

"It was one of the luckiest hits of my life that I met him. He mingled but little with the public, but was widely known for his remarkable intelligence and incorruptible integrity, and for a heart brimful and running over with kindness and benevolence, which showed themselves not only in words but in acts. He was the oracle of the whole country around him, and his fame had extended far beyond the circle of his immediate acquaintance. Though I had never met him before, I had heard much of him, and but for this meeting it is very likely I should have had opposition, and had been beaten. One thing is very certain, no man could now stand up in that district under such a vote.

"At the appointed time I was at his house, having told our conversation to every crowd I had met, and to every man I stayed all night with, and I found that it gave the people an interest and a confidence in me stronger than I had every seen manifested before.

"Though I was considerably fatigued when I reached his house, and, under ordinary circumstances, should have gone early to bed, I kept him up until midnight, talking about the principles and affairs of government, and got more real, true knowledge of them than I had got all my life before.

"I have known and seen much of him since, for I respect him–no, that is not the word–I reverence and love him more than any living man, and I go to see him two or three times every year; and I will tell you, sir, if every one who professes to be a Christian lived and acted and enjoyed it as he does, the religion of Christ would take the world by storm.

"But to return to my story. The next morning we went to the barbecue, and, to my surprise, found about a thousand men there. I met a good many whom I had not known before, and they and my friend introduced me around until I had got pretty well acquainted–at least, they all knew me.

"In due time notice was given that I would speak to them. They gathered up around a stand that had been erected. I opened my speech by saying:

"'Fellow-citizens–I present myself before you today feeling like a new man. My eyes have lately been opened to truths which ignorance or prejudice, or both, had heretofore hidden from my view. I feel that I can today offer you the ability to render you more valuable service than I have ever been able to render before. I am here today more for the purpose of acknowledging my error than to seek your votes. That I should make this acknowledgment is due to myself as well as to you. Whether you will vote for me is a matter for your consideration only.'

"I went on to tell them about the fire and my vote for the appropriation and then told them why I was satisfied it was wrong. I closed by saying:

"'And now, fellow-citizens, it remains only for me to tell you that the most of the speech you have listened to with so much interest was simply a repetition of the arguments by which your neighbor, Mr. Bunce, convinced me of my error.

"'It is the best speech I ever made in my life, but he is entitled to the credit for it. And now I hope he is satisfied with his convert and that he will get up here and tell you so.'

"He came upon the stand and said:

"'Fellow-citizens–It affords me great pleasure to comply with the request of Colonel Crockett. I have always considered him a thoroughly honest man, and I am satisfied that he will faithfully perform all that he has promised you today.'

"He went down, and there went up from that crowd such a shout for Davy Crockett as his name never called forth before.

"I am not much given to tears, but I was taken with a choking then and felt some big drops rolling down my cheeks. And I tell you now that the remembrance of those few words spoken by such a man, and the honest, hearty shout they produced, is worth more to me than all the honors I have received and all the reputation I have ever made, or ever shall make, as a member of Congress.

"Now, sir," concluded Crockett, "you know why I made that speech yesterday.

"There is one thing now to which I will call your attention. You remember that I proposed to give a week's pay. There are in that House many very wealthy men–men who think nothing of spending a week's pay, or a dozen of them, for a dinner or a wine party when they have something to accomplish by it. Some of those same men made beautiful speeches upon the great debt of gratitude which the country owed the deceased–a debt which could not be paid by money–and the insignificance and worthlessness of money, particularly so insignificant a sum as $10,000, when weighted against the honor of the nation. Yet not one of them responded to my proposition. Money with them is nothing but trash when it is to come out of the people. But it is the one great thing for which most of them are striving, and many of them sacrifice honor, integrity, and justice to obtain it."

Holders of political office are but reflections of the dominant leadership–good or bad–among the electorate.

Horatio Bunce is a striking example of responsible citizenship. Were his kind to multiply, we would see many new faces in public office; or, as in the case of Davy Crockett, a new Crockett.

For either the new faces or the new Crocketts, we must look to the Horatio in ourselves!"

(For more information about Davy Crockett and the "Not Yours to Give Speech", see Jim Boylston's blog post about the subject at http://crockettincongress.blogspot.com/2009/10/not-yours-to-give-fable-re-examined.html)

Chapter 10: Bowie's Legacy

Homage

Bowie, Texas, Bowie County, Texas, and Bowie Street in Downtown San Antonio are all named in honor of James Jim Bowie.

At the "1988 Blade Show" in Atlanta, Georgia, Jim Bowie was inducted posthumously into the *Blade Magazine* Cutlery Hall of Fame in recognition of the impact the Bowie knife had on generations of knife makers and cutlery companies.

Around 1820, the only known image of Jim Bowie created during his lifetime was produced, an oil painting attributed to American artist George Peter Alexander Healy. Doubt is cast on its creator, however, in an 1889 letter by then owner John Moore, who stated, "Photograph of Col. Jas. Bowie taken from his portrait painting by West." Although Moore does not indicate West's first name, this probably would be Kentucky-born William Edward West (1788-1857), who is known to have painted the portraits of several prominent figures and worked in New Orleans in 1818. A copy of this portrait hangs on the south wall of the Texas Capitol House of Representatives Chamber, painted in 1894 by Mamie Cardwell while the original was the property of Jim Bowie's grand-nephew, Major John S. Moore of New Orleans. On June 26, 2001, it was purchased for the State of Texas at auction.

Perspective

Perhaps more than any other popular figure in American history, the legacy surrounding Jim Bowie has been established by speculation, romanticizing, and iconic immortalizing based more on legend than factual information. While often categorized with frontiersmen like Daniel Boone and Davy Crockett, in actuality Bowie's story has from the beginning grown more from larger-than-life legend than documented deeds, and Bowie has far less tangible accomplishments than Boone (who played a vital role in colonizing Kentucky) and Crockett (who was a Congressman).

Despite his continual pronouncements of wealth during his lifetime, Bowie's estate was found to be quite small; his possessions were said to have fetched a mere $99.50 at auction even despite his fame at the time of his death. As historian J. R. Edmonton points out, regardless of his larger legacy being that of one of the legendary characters of the American frontier, Bowie left a "frustratingly sparse paper trail" of his life, and "where history failed, the legends prevailed."[23]

And though Bowie's name and trademark knife were well known across America (and even Europe, where kids are said to have idolized the Alamo defender) during his lifetime, his legend grew exponentially after October 1852 when *DeBow's Review* published an article written by his brother John Bowie called "Early Life in the Southwest—The Bowies." Following that article, which was a mixture of fact and fable that focused primarily on the exploits of Jim Bowie, "romanticized stories" about Bowie began to appear with increasing frequency in national newspapers and periodicals. In many cases, "these stories were pure melodrama, with Bowie rescuing some naïve planter's son or damsel in distress."[24]

While Jim Bowie's physical image has been largely distorted by tall tales of knife fights and desperate run-ins with "Indians," pirates, and Mexican soldiers alike, the lone portrait that survives him would seem to support the description provided by his brother John who described him as "a stout, rather raw-boned man, of six feet height, weighed 180 pounds . . . with light-colored hair, keen grey eyes rather deep set in his head, a fair complexion, and high cheekbones."[25]

Famously fond of hunting and fishing, family tradition characterizes him as having caught and rode wild horses, trapped bears, and even rode alligators, all of which are likely more fable than fact. While his brother John describes him as having an "open, frank disposition, but when aroused by an insult, his anger was terrible," he is also thought to have been well traveled and generous, but a man of extraordinary ambition—scheming and by some accounts, a card sharp and cheat. He apparently lived most of his life in debt, and he was always contriving how to get out of it.

When newspapers picked up the story that came to be known as the "Sandbar Fight" (in some circles, the "Great Sandbar Duel"), Jim Bowie's fighting prowess and the knife he used so proficiently was described in detail. Eyewitness accounts agree that Bowie did not attack first and that the others had focused their attack on him specifically because "they considered him the most dangerous man among their opposition", though no one seemed to know what precipitated the unprovoked attack in the first place.

After the "Sandbar Fight" and other alleged confrontations in which Bowie successfully used his knife to defend himself, his unique blade became very popular. Although many people today know of Jim Bowie's participation at the Alamo, the name "Bowie" is most closely associated with creation and manufacture of the "Bowie Knife." Described as one of the most "dangerously

---

[23] Edmondson, J. R. *The Alamo Story-From History to Current Conflicts*. Page 119.

[24] Edmondson, J. R. *The Alamo Story-From History to Current Conflicts*. Page 119.

[25] Edmondson, J. R. *The Alamo Story-From History to Current Conflicts*. Page 118.

effective" hunting knives ever created, Bowie is said to have conceived of the long, trademark "bolster" (the perpendicular metal piece adjoining the handle to a then-standard butcher knife to make it a more user-friendly weapon). Other accounts credit Bowie with the creation of the first modified model. While most blades of the era were designed primarily for utilitarian, practical uses, the "Bowie" was designed firstly as a combat weapon, said to have been prompted after Jim lost his grip on a butcher knife during an "Indian" fight.

First manufactured for sale about 1825, production of the "Bowie" is credited to James Black, a Washington, Arkansas blacksmith said to have taken Jim Bowie's original design and married it to a new method of tempering steel that made blades far sharp than ever before. Nicknamed the "Arkansas toothpick" by mountaineers of that state, early pioneers routinely carried the "Bowie" for skinning deer (and hand-to-hand defense against hostile Native—and White--Americans when need be), with Texas Rangers said to have depended on the knife as much as their sidearms. And of course, due to its legendary lethality, Mississippi River pirates, highwaymen (known as "road agents"), and others of the "criminal element" found it quite useful. Beyond a doubt, at one point in American history, it was the most popular blade in the country. (During World War II, both American and British commandos carried versions of the "Bowie.")

As one of the most prominent tools of the American frontier, the "Bowie" (still prized today although new designs and materials have relegated it more of a *preference*) is 10-15 inches long, nearly two inches wide, and has a curved, hand-crafted single-edge blade; a horn handle; and its then-distinctive sword-hilt-like *bolster*. The prominent bolster not only provides additional grip and control but also strengthens the knife, adds durability, and provides counter-balance.

Naturally, there is some dispute as to whether or not Jim Bowie ever got to use the actual knife bearing his name, since it is likely his brother had a prototype crafted for him and others suggest he merely carried a modified butcher knife. Moreover, many craftsmen and manufacturers made their own versions of it, with many major cities of the Southwest opening "Bowie knife schools" that taught the art of cut, thrust, and parry, essential to defending oneself with a knife. By the early 1830s, Jim Bowie's fame and that of his equally famous knife had spread to England, with several British knife manufacturers subsequently producing Bowie knives, which were exported to the United States.

After the fall of the Alamo, three names spread across America as if they were themselves on fire: Davy Crockett, William Travis, and Jim Bowie. Portrayed as an infallible, iconic hero, the American public romanticized Bowie in a manner few before him had been afforded, with his notorious flaws and shortcomings quickly falling into the shadow of his spotlight. He and his famous knife made his slave-trading, fraudulent land dealings and property swindling vanish from his reputation, as well as his relinquishing of his United States citizenship and deceitful conversion to Catholicism. Before the Alamo, these were the most important details of Bowie's life, but they have since gone virtually unnoticed.

While many historians dispute most common legends surrounding Jim Bowie, few have been able to provide documentation to the contrary. In his 2000 book, *The Alamo Story: From History to Current Conflicts*, historian and author J. R. Edmondson attempts to clear up some of the myths surrounding Bowie. Edmondson debunks the common contention that Bowie fell and broke his hip while at the Alamo, and he also reveals that the location of the "Sandbar Fight" was not on the Vidalia sandbar as has been reported in other books; the actual location was Giles Island on the Louisiana side of the Natchez River.

Pop Culture

"Bowie" (perhaps the man, perhaps the knife) was taken as the stage-name of rock star David Bowie (born David Robert Hayward-Jones in 1947) in the 1960s, fearing that his name was too similar to pop star Davy Jones of the famous *The Monkees*.

A number of films have depicted the fateful events at the Battle of the Alamo, with Jim Bowie playing a prominent role in each.

In the 1955 film *The Last Command,* Jim Bowie (played by Sterling Hayden) is the main character during the Battle of the Alamo and the Texas War of Independence.

In the 1952 film *The Iron Mistress,* the role of Jim Bowie is played actor Alan Ladd.

In the now-classic 1960 John Wayne vehicle, *The Alamo*, film star Richard Widmark portrays Jim Bowie.

In the 2004 remake of *The Alamo*, Jason Patric plays Bowie.

From 1956 to 1958, Jim Bowie was the subject of the American television show, *The Adventures of Jim Bowie*, which was set primarily in 1830s Louisiana, although later episodes ventured into the Mexican province of Texas. The show, with Scott Forbes in the starring role, was based on the 1946 Monte Barrett novel, *Tempered Blade*.

Bowie Bibliography

The Alamo.org website: http://thealamo.org/battle/battle.php accessed 10.06.2012.

Batson, James L. *James Bowie and the Sandbar Fight*. Madison, Alabama: Batson Engineering and Metalworks, 1992.

Classic TV and Movie website, *The Adventures of Jim Bowie*:
http://www.classictvhits.com/show.php?id=397 accessed 10.06.2012.

Davis, William C. *Three Roads to the Alamo*. New York: HarperCollins, 1998.

Edmondson, J. R. *The Alamo Story-From History to Current Conflicts*. Plano, TX: Republic of Texas Press, 2000.

Historic Kansas Museum, "James Black and the Bowie Knife."
http://www.historicarkansas.org/knife_gallery/ accessed 10.05.2012.

Hopewell, Clifford. *James Bowie Texas Fighting Man: A Biography*. Austin, TX: Eakin Press, 1994.

Los Almagres, the Lost Spanish Mine website:
http://www.texasbeyondhistory.net/plateaus/images/he13.html accessed 10.06.2012.

State Preservation Board website, "Jim Bowie Portrait."
http://www.tspb.state.tx.us/spb/gallery/HisArt/01.htm accessed 10.07.2012.

Texas State Historical Association, *The Handbook of Texas Online*, "Bowie, James."
http://www.tshaonline.org/handbook/online/articles/fbo45 accessed 10.05.2012.

Wallis, Michael. *David Crockett: The Lion of the West*. New York: W. W. Norton & Company, 2011.

Crockett Bibliography

The Alamo.org website: http://thealamo.org/battle/battle.php accessed 08.30.2012.

Blair, Walter. *David Crockett: Legendary Frontier Hero*. IL: Lincoln-Herndon Press, 1986.

Garland, Hamlin, (ed.). *The Autobiography of Davy Crockett*. New York: Charles Scribner's Sons, 1923.

Petite, Mary Deborah. *Facts about the Alamo and the Texas War for Independence*. Mason City, IA: Savas Publishing Company, 1999.

Project Gutenberg eBook, "A Narrative of the Life of David Crockett, of the State of Tennessee, by Davy Crockett," accessed via http://www.gutenberg.org/files/37925/37925-h/37925-h.htm 08.31.2012.

Virginia.edu website: http://etext.virginia.edu/railton/projects/price/acrocket.htm.

Wallis, Michael. *David Crockett: The Lion of the West*. New York: W. W. Norton & Company, 2011.

Made in the USA
Columbia, SC
16 January 2025